First Time Mom and Baby Sleep Guide 2-in-1 Book

Monthly Pregnancy Guide to Learn What is Coming in The Next 9 Months and Discover the Secrets of Baby Sleep to Enjoy a Rested, Joyful Motherhood

Pregnancy

A New Mom's Survival Handbook With All the Helpful Tips & Information You Need While Expecting + 30 Day Meal Plan for Pregnancy

Table of Contents

Introduction 7
Chapter 1 - The Journey Begins.. 10
   An Essential Quit List for All Pregnant Women 10
   The Truth About Weight Gain During Pregnancy....................... 14
   What About Stretch Marks? 16
   5 Health-Boosting Supplements for Mom and Baby 18
Chapter 2 - The First Trimester.. 22
   10 Common Symptoms of the First Trimester & How to Manage Them 23
   When to Call Your Doctor... 27
   5 Ways Your Body Will Change in the First Trimester 28
   What is a Doula & How Can They Help? 30
Chapter 3 - The Second Trimester.. 33
   Pelvic Floor Exercises that All Mothers Must Know 33
   5 Ways to Start Bonding With Your Baby 35
   Watch Out For These Signs of Preeclampsia 37
   The Best Ways to Exercise in the Second Trimester.................... 38
   10 Fun Ideas for the Second Trimester 40
Chapter 4 - The Third Trimester.. 44
   Every First-Time Mom's To-Do List for the Third Trimester 44
   Breastfeeding vs. Formula Feeding 47

Tackling Third-Trimester Insomnia 49
Labor Signals & What They Mean 50
Braxton Hicks Contractions vs. Labor Contractions..................... 52
How Do You Induce Labor Safely and Naturally? 53

Chapter 5 - Preparing for the Big Day..55
Pack These 13 Essentials in Your Hospital Bag 55
22 New-Baby & First-Time Mom Necessities.............................. 58
How to Start Creating a Birth Plan.. 66

Chapter 6 - Childbirth & Labor..69
10 Less-Known Things You Should Know About Vaginal Childbirth & Labor... 69
4 Things to Do for a Safer C-Section.. 73
The Lowdown on Epidural Anesthesia 73
7 Helpful Tricks for Pushing that Baby Out 75
The Best Positions for Pushing with an Epidural.......................... 76
7 Little-Known Things about C-Sections 77

Chapter 7 - Postpartum Care 79
What Every Mother Needs to Do after Giving Birth 79
9 Completely Normal Long-Term & Short-Term Effects of Pregnancy and Childbirth... 80
How to Help the Body Heal from Birth 84
Everything You Need to Know About Postpartum Depression.... 86
9 Soul-Soothing Self-Care Ideas for a First-Time Mom............... 87

Chapter 8 - Your Newborn Baby 91

11 Things You Should Know About Newborn Babies 91

6 Must-Know Rules About Formula-Feeding 93

Foods to Limit or Avoid While Breastfeeding 94

How to Prevent Sudden Infant Death Syndrome 96

It's Bath Time! 99

Conclusion 103

30 Day Meal Plan 106

    Week 1 106

    Week 2 107

    Week 3 109

    Week 4 110

    Week 5 112

    Snack List 114

Introduction

You're about to become a mother for the first time – congratulations! These months will be some of the most special in your entire life and also, some of the most challenging. As overjoyed as you are to be bringing a new life into the world, chances are you're also incredibly nervous. Carrying a child is no walk in the park, as you've likely heard. And when it's your first time, it's all new and uncertain territory. You're probably anxious about the ways your body is changing, the new sensations you're experiencing, and above all, you're wondering how on earth you can keep your baby healthy when there is such an overload of information about what to do and not do. If you're feeling overwhelmed by this new chapter in your life, no one would blame you.

Thing is, pregnancy does not have to be a time of confusion and anxiety. This may be an entirely new experience, but that doesn't mean it has to be fraught with worry. All you need is the right guidance and helpful, accurate information that is easily accessible to you at all times. With this book by your side, you can transition confidently into your role as a first-time mom. Each chapter will guide you through the many steps of your pregnancy, so you'll never feel uncertain. No more stress or anxiety. Just total awareness and all the preparation you need to be the most competent mom for your new baby.

In this book, each trimester will be completely demystified. I'll get in-depth about each specific trimester and what your baby needs from you in each one. You'll understand your symptoms, how to manage them, activities to avoid at all costs, what to eat for your baby's optimal health, how to prepare for labor and birth – and so much more. If you have a question, I have an answer. Just take a peek in this book whenever you're not sure about something.

Pregnancy Guide

As the proud mom of five beautiful and healthy children, it's safe to say I am very experienced when it comes to pregnancy and baby care. I vividly remember what it was like to be pregnant for the first time – I devoured a heap of books, frustrated that I couldn't find *just one book* to cover everything. For over a decade I coached friends through their first pregnancies, began the popular 'Happy Mom, Happy Baby' club in my hometown, and of course, I expanded my knowledge as each of my other babies came along. No two pregnancies are alike – but what I've learned is that the best advice and support always comes from an experienced mom.

With the best advice under your belt, you'll ride the waves of pregnancy with confidence. You can focus on your own physical and emotional well-being so that, when your baby comes, he or she is brought into the best possible environment. No mom will tell you that pregnancy is easy, but what it *can* be is a clarifying and empowering experience for the lifetime of motherhood that is to come. With this book, you'll have all the tools you need to get on the right path.

The people I coach and the friends I've supported through first-time pregnancies continue to thank me to this day. While every mom knows there's no such thing as a pregnancy 'expert,' I've been told I come as close as you can get. The secrets I share with the people I help are exactly what I will be unveiling in this book. You, too, can reap the benefits I've seen other mothers blossom with.

When it comes to your pregnancy preparation, there's no such thing as doing it later. Your budding baby needs specific conditions *now*; you're either preparing or you're not. The early days are some of the most crucial for your baby's development, as you are still at risk of a miscarriage. Make sure you get the right help as soon as possible, so you can get your baby on the path towards optimal health.

Pregnancy Guide

The chance to be a good mom doesn't just arise when your baby is born; the chance is here already. It is now. The choices you make while your child is in your belly have the potential to affect his or her entire life. Don't stumble into motherhood. Take strong, empowered steps. As you turn the page, feel assured that the first strong step begins.

Chapter 1 - The Journey Begins

With a decade of pregnancy coaching behind me, I've noticed many similarities between all first-time moms, especially in the early days. Once the thrill and joy from their good news has settled, they have the same concerns. "How much do I have to change my current lifestyle?" is the general gist of most of their questions. They ask me, "How can I stop myself from gaining so much weight?" or "How can I prevent stretch marks?" New moms tend to feel guilty for asking these questions, but there's no reason to! A baby changes everything and that includes your body. It's okay to have moments where you feel overwhelmed – where it feels like the world is shifting under your feet. Be patient with yourself and know that it's a lot easier to navigate when you take it one step at a time.

In this chapter, I'll cover all the first concerns that I've heard from first-time moms. Everything you need to know right off the bat is here, as it'll likely apply to your entire pregnancy. The journey has begun – embrace it!

An Essential Quit List for All Pregnant Women

When you're pregnant, the last thing you should be doing is business as usual. You are no longer the only person affected by your diet and habits; there's a new life on board now. And in some cases, 'business as usual' can have disastrous consequences on the new life you're creating. Once you know you're expecting, you'll need to cull every single habit that's on this quit list. This is non-negotiable. It's absolutely essential that you and your baby are safe and healthy.

1. Smoking and Second-Hand Smoke

Pregnancy Guide

Smoking can have an extremely negative impact on your baby's health and your pregnancy as a whole. Pregnant women who smoke are much more likely to have a miscarriage, go through premature labor, or an ectopic pregnancy. And believe it or not, second-hand smoke is just as harmful. Exposure can lead to the same consequences as smoking and may even result in behavioral or learning issues in the growing child.

2. Chores that Involve Strong Chemicals and Fumes

Pregnant women don't get a free pass on all household chores but you should definitely avoid duties that involve heavy chemicals such as oven cleaners, aerosol products, and pesticides. It's difficult to steer clear of all chemicals – so if you're unsure if what you're using is safe, read the warning label and instructions. If you're the sole cleaner of the house, consider turning to natural options like baking soda and vinegar which can often do an equally efficient job. In addition to this, always wear rubber gloves when handling cleaning products and make sure a few windows are open so your home gets excellent ventilation. These practices can make all the difference!

3. All Alcohol

By now, quitting alcohol is well-known as an essential part of a healthy pregnancy – and for good reasons! When a pregnant woman drinks alcohol, it reaches her baby. This is because alcohol can pass through the bloodstream into the placenta. This can damage the baby's brain and organs, resulting in birth defects, brain damage, stillbirth, a miscarriage, and more. All types of alcohol must be avoided during pregnancy, including wine, beer, and liquor.

4. Over 200mg of Caffeine

You don't need to give up coffee or green tea entirely when you're expecting – but you should avoid consuming large amounts. Too much caffeine puts women at a higher risk of miscarriage. On top of this, studies have shown that caffeine can enter the placenta; this means that when you ingest caffeine, so does your baby. Caffeine may just give *you* a light buzz, but think of the effect it can have on a newly formed being without a developed metabolism. If you're a coffee drinker, limit yourself to one cup a day and no more. Keep in mind that many sodas and energy drinks also contain caffeine. If you enjoy drinking these types of beverages, pay close attention to how much caffeine they contain.

5. High-Mercury Fish

Fish can be highly beneficial for a pregnant woman's diet, but high-mercury fish are a whole different deal. Women who are pregnant or nursing are advised to steer clear of fish with high amounts of mercury in their meat. This means no tuna, shark, mackerel, and swordfish.

6. Unpasteurized Dairy Products

Pregnant women *and* infants should steer clear of unpasteurized dairy. In other words, anything made from raw milk such as unpasteurized cheese and obviously, raw milk itself. The pasteurization process kills harmful bacteria – so when you consume raw milk, there's a possibility it could contain dangerous microorganisms with the potential to pose life-threatening consequences to you and your child. A study published by the Minnesota Department of Public Health revealed that one in six people who drink raw milk will get sick. It is advised that all pregnant women play it safe and avoid consuming all forms of raw milk from any animal.

7. Cleaning Cat Litter

If you own a cat, pass the cat litter-cleaning duties to your partner, family member, or other housemates. As adorable as your cat is, he or she could be a carrier of the *Toxoplasma Gondii* parasite which could be transferred to you through contact with your cat's waste. This parasite can cause an infection called Toxoplasmosis and if you're infected while pregnant, it can result in big problems for the baby or your pregnancy, such as stillbirth or miscarriage. If there's no one else to change the cat litter, then take extra precautions by wearing gloves, only feeding your cat dry food, washing your hands thoroughly afterward and keeping your cat indoors.

8. Heavy-Lifting

Pregnant women should avoid all forms of heavy-lifting, as the strain caused can do different types of damage, depending on the trimester. In the first trimester, straining to lift heavy-objects may trigger a miscarriage. In later trimesters, the risks only increase. Due to hormone changes during pregnancy, the ligaments in a woman's pelvic floor and joints loosen; this makes them more prone to damage and stress. A weakened pelvic floor can lead to big problems with incontinence (inability to control urination) or even potentially lead to the womb collapsing into the vagina (prolapse). Although some women are more at risk than overs, a general rule of thumb is to avoid heavy lifting altogether and get someone to help you.

9. Some Types of Exercise

Exercise is highly recommended for all pregnant women, but certain types should be avoided. The following exercises present a variety of risks and are not suitable for pregnant women:

- Anything that involves jumping, bouncing, or leaping.
- Exercises with jerky movements or sudden direction changes.
- Contact sports such as soccer, boxing, basketball, or ice hockey.

- Abdominal exercises that involve lying on the back.
- Exercises that require lying on the stomach.
- Activities with a fall risk such as rock-climbing, skiing, gymnastics, and horseback riding.

10. Certain Over-the-Counter Medications

Pregnant women are advised against taking medication they used before pregnancy unless they speak to a doctor about it first. Many seemingly harmless over-the-counter medications, such as aspirin or ibuprofen, are incredibly risky during pregnancy. In the first trimester, they can bring about miscarriage and later on, they can lead to birth defects in your baby. A good rule of thumb is to always talk to your doctor before you use any type of medicine.

The Truth About Weight Gain During Pregnancy

It is well-known that weight gain should be expected during pregnancy. While the amount of weight gained will vary from woman to woman, there are many who gain a tremendous amount of weight and unfortunately, this prospect can worry some new mothers. Of course, new mothers shouldn't worry about how much weight they're gaining; as long as they and their babies are healthy, that's all that matters. Still, it's completely understandable if some moms want to watch their weight and in some cases, it may be advised.

Most mothers will not be obese during their pregnancy, which is the only time weight gain can become a significant risk. Mothers who are obese are at an increased risk of preeclampsia, gestational diabetes, and premature birth. So if you were already overweight prior to becoming pregnant, pay close attention to the following facts.

- You don't need extra calories in your first and second trimester

Pregnancy Guide

We've all heard the phrase 'eating for two' used in conjunction with a pregnant woman, but unknown to most, this does not refer to the amount of food eaten. Pregnant women do not need to eat twice as much in the first and second trimester. It's not calories they need more of, but nutrients. Instead of eating larger amounts, they need to be focusing on more nutrient-rich foods. The misconception around 'eating for two' can lead to a lot of needless weight gain.

- How much weight you need to gain depends on your starting weight

The average woman needs to gain between 25 and 35 lbs for a healthy pregnancy but some may need to gain less or more, depending on how much they already weigh. The less you currently weigh, the more you'll need to gain and the more you weigh, the less you'll need to gain. Those who are underweight will need to gain between 28 and 40 lbs, while those who are overweight should only gain between 15 to 25 lbs. If you're pregnant with more than one baby, expect these numbers to be higher.

- Weight is not just fat

Weight gain is crucial for your pregnancy and that's because you're not just gaining fat. In fact, if a woman gains 35 lbs during pregnancy, only 5 to 9 lbs will consist of fat stores. Increased breast tissue, blood supply, uterus growth, amniotic fluid, the placenta, and of course, the baby itself all take up that extra weight. Putting on less weight could mean giving your baby less of what it needs to be completely healthy – so don't try to put on less than your recommended weight.

- Weight gain isn't consistent

You won't gain weight steadily throughout your pregnancy. You'll go many weeks remaining at a consistent weight but you'll also see times, usually in the second trimester, where weight gain happens very rapidly. And later in the third trimester, as you approach your due date, all weight gain will come to a halt.

- Safe exercise can keep excess fat off

Not only will it help with weight gain, but it can also relieve aches and pains during the latter part of pregnancy. The important thing is that exercise isn't too strenuous. The perfect way to stay active is by making walking a part of your routine. Doctors recommend starting with at least ten minutes of walking a day and adding ten minutes every month. And remember, the walking you do while running errands counts too! If you enjoyed jogging before you were pregnant, feel free to continue doing this.

What About Stretch Marks?

When skin stretches due to rapid weight gain, this can result in stretch marks. Over the course of pregnancy, women may get stretch marks on their belly, breasts, thighs, upper arms, and sometimes even on their buttocks. Fresh stretch marks often appear slightly red or purple but as they get older, they'll fade to a white or silver color.

Unfortunately, there is no sure way to avoid stretch marks completely. Nine out of ten women get them to some degree during pregnancy. Genetics will also play a big role in determining whether you get stretch marks and their appearance. If your parents or grandparents developed stretch marks, you're more likely to as well.

Even if you're genetically predisposed to get stretch marks, there are steps you can take to lower your chances. The following practices have proven to help with minimizing and preventing stretch marks:

Get Enough Vitamin D

Pregnancy Guide

Studies have shown that low levels of vitamin D can increase the likelihood of getting stretch marks. To increase your levels of this important vitamin, consider eating foods fortified with vitamin D (many types of cereal, milk or yogurt) or getting more sun exposure.

Stay Moisturized

Stretch marks are far more likely to appear on dry skin – so to stave them off, make sure to keep your skin moisturized. Consider using brands such as Mederma, Earth Mama, or Bio-Oil which have all been known to help with existing stretch marks as well as prevention.

Stay Hydrated

Moisturizing on the outside is one thing, but increasing your water intake and moisture-levels inside can be far more beneficial for stretch mark prevention. When your body is fully hydrated, your skin softens and is, therefore, much less prone to developing stretch marks. Women with dry skin will find it a lot more difficult to avoid scarring from weight gain.

Get Lots of Vitamin C

Stretch marks or not, vitamin C is known to be highly beneficial in the pursuit of healthy skin. This is because vitamin C plays a crucial role in your body's production of collagen – an important protein responsible for your skin's elasticity. To boost your levels of vitamin C, eat more fruit and veg or consider taking a vitamin C supplement.

Control Your Pregnancy Weight

A mother should never limit her nutrient intake in pursuit of being smaller-sized, but mothers *can* limit the amount of food they eat. Focus on small but frequent meals, rich with all the nutrients you need. And when you can, try to stave off cravings for unhealthy food!

Treat Stretch Marks as Soon as They Appear

The sooner you treat stretch marks, the higher the likelihood of improving their appearance. Once you see purple or red marks forming, make sure to lather on a reliable stretch mark-control product or moisturizer. For the best luck, you'll need to treat the affected area daily even if you don't see results as fast as you want to. Even those who moisturize diligently can end up waiting a month to see big improvements.

5 Health-Boosting Supplements for Mom and Baby

As soon as you become pregnant, your body starts to demand more nutrients. This is true of macronutrients such as protein, fat, and carbohydrates, but it is especially true for micronutrients, which include vitamins and minerals. To make sure you're meeting this growing demand, it's recommended that women either commit to eating a nutrient-rich diet or at the very least, make supplements a part of their daily routine. If you're experiencing strong aversions to food or nausea during your pregnancy, you're going to want to keep a stock of these supplements so you're still getting the nutrients you need.

In addition to these supplements, make sure you talk to your doctor about the best prenatal vitamins for you to take. Your prenatal vitamins will cover a decent chunk of your nutrient requirements, but not everything. It's always best to see what your prenatal vitamins give you and what you need to get most of elsewhere.

Please note that all the supplements on this list have been deemed safe by medical health professionals. If you're considering taking a supplement that is not on this list, speak to a doctor before doing so.

Folic Acid

Recommended Amount: 600 mcg

Natural Sources: Asparagus, eggs, beets, avocado, spinach, broccoli.

Pregnancy Guide

Vitamin B9, commonly known as Folic Acid, is well-known for being vital to a growing baby's development and overall health. Numerous studies have shown that folic acid is directly responsible for reducing the risk of certain birth defects and abnormalities. Doctors even recommend a folate supplement for women trying to get pregnant, as intake before pregnancy brings even more benefits. Although it is possible, most women do not eat enough folate through their diet alone so a supplement can help greatly.

Vitamin D

Recommended Amount: 50 mcg

Natural Sources: sunlight, fatty fish such as salmon or mackerel, egg yolks, foods fortified with vitamin D including dairy and some cereals.

Vitamin D deficiency is, unfortunately, very common, not just in pregnant women but all people. In pregnancy, an inadequate intake of vitamin D has been linked to bone fractures, abnormal bone growth, preeclampsia, bacterial vaginosis, and rickets in newborns. Vitamin D is an essential nutrient for all pregnant women as it plays a prominent role in building your baby's bones and teeth. Unlike most other vitamin deficiencies, it is possible to be vitamin D deficient and display no obvious symptoms.

Iron

Recommended Amount: 27 mg

Natural Sources: oysters, clams, mussels, chicken or beef liver, spinach.

Your maternal blood volume will increase by 50% during pregnancy, so this means your need for iron will as well. Iron has proven to be crucial in the healthy development of both the fetus and the placenta. Iron deficiency, or anemia, has been linked to a higher risk of infant anemia, preterm delivery and even depression for the mother-to-be. With iron, it's important that only the recommended intake is consumed and not more than that. Too much iron can induce vomiting, constipation, and many other unpleasant side effects.

Magnesium

Recommended Amount: 310 mg

Natural Sources: Dark chocolate, avocado, almonds, cashews, tofu, pumpkin seeds, flax seeds, spinach.

A woman's requirement for magnesium increases during pregnancy, and since it gets excreted in larger amounts through urine or vomiting (morning sickness), it is advised that mothers replenish their magnesium levels through their diet or supplementation. Studies have shown that a magnesium deficiency in pregnant women leads to a higher risk of preterm birth, preeclampsia, and fetal growth restriction. Sufficient levels, however, have been linked to reduced cramping while pregnant and, believe it or not, newborns with better sleep cycles!

Iodine

Recommended Amount: 260 mcg

Natural Sources: Cod, plain yogurt, cottage cheese, shrimp, eggs.

Our daily requirement for iodine is extremely tiny in comparison to other vitamins and minerals – but that tiny amount is very important. In pregnant women, iodine assists the thyroid in regulating hormones that control your heart rate, metabolism, and other functions. Mothers who do not get enough iodine significantly increase the risk of their baby being born with an underdeveloped thyroid. This can lead to a child with deafness, birth defects, learning disabilities, a low IQ, and much more. Since too much iodine can also pose serious risks, doctors recommend taking an iodine supplement with only 150 mcg and no more.

Before we dive into the first trimester, please keep in mind that everything in this chapter applies to the entire pregnancy. Make good habits part of your daily routine and eventually, both you and your baby will reap the benefits!

Chapter 2 - The First Trimester

Did you know the first trimester begins before you're even pregnant? Unknown to most, Day 1 is not the day of conception, but instead the first day of your last period before becoming pregnant. The first trimester lasts from this day until the end of week 12. When a woman discovers she is pregnant, she's usually five or six weeks into her pregnancy already. By this point, a heartbeat can usually be detected. Believe it or not, your baby grows the most rapidly in the first trimester than in any other trimester. More changes happen in such a short space of time than at any other point in your pregnancy. Curious about what these changes are? Here are some of the biggest developments of the first trimester:

- The fertilized egg has implanted itself into your womb – where it'll continue to grow for the next eight to nine months.
- The embryo will start dividing into three layers. The topmost layer will eventually form your baby's skin, eyes, and ears. The middle layer will become your baby's bones, kidneys, ligaments, and most of their reproductive system. And from the bottom layer, your baby's other organs such as the lungs and intestines will begin to develop.
- By the time week 12 rolls around, your baby's muscles and bones have formed, as well as all the organs of their body. It has a distinguishable human form and can now officially be called a fetus.

As these big developments take place, a mother's body starts to experience a lot of new feelings. You're likely going through some of these already. Rest assured, it's all part of the process that is the formation of life.

Pregnancy Guide

10 Common Symptoms of the First Trimester & How to Manage Them

You'll start feeling pregnant long before you start looking pregnant. It may be the early days but the first trimester is still fraught with its own set of symptoms. When you don't know what to expect, it can be difficult to distinguish between what's normal and what isn't. Not every mother will experience the symptoms on this list – in fact, you may even find that it varies with each pregnancy you have. If you're experiencing any of the following symptoms, know that it's completely normal and most mothers will tick off at least a box or two. And best of all, there is some degree of relief available.

1. Morning Sickness

There isn't just one cause for morning sickness, but it's largely due to rising hormone levels. Unfortunately, the term 'morning sickness' is rather misleading. Pregnancy-related nausea and vomiting can hit you at any time of the day, typically starting after week 6. As awful as you may feel, doctors do not advise skipping meals; in fact, you may find yourself feeling even worse on an empty stomach. Instead, just limit yourself to small meals, drink plenty of fluids, and sip on some stomach-soothing ginger tea. If nausea persists, consider getting some acupressure wristbands. Thankfully, morning sickness tends to subside by the second trimester.

2. Fatigue

Your body is making a lot of adjustments and changes to accommodate a baby, and naturally, this can result in extreme tiredness. Sometimes the best thing to do is to just let yourself relax and lay down, as you please. Now's the time for self-care. Curl up on the sofa and read, watch TV, or do whatever it is you enjoy doing in your spare time. If you're frustrated with being sedentary all the time, consider adding energy-boosting foods to your diet. Some of these include sweet potatoes, spinach, and oatmeal. And while you're at it, make sure you're drinking enough water as dehydration can add to pregnancy fatigue.

3. Constipation

It's normal to have more trouble than usual with bowel movements while pregnant. If you're not exercising or drinking enough water, this can contribute to the problem. It's also common knowledge that certain prenatal vitamins can make constipation even worse. If the problem persists after hydrating and exercising more often, you may want to speak to your doctor about switching to different vitamins.

4. Aversions to Certain Foods

Due to hormonal changes, you're likely to feel completely repulsed by certain foods. This is usually linked to feelings of morning sickness. Some of the foods you'll feel averse to may include spicy food, meat (especially red), garlic, milk and any others that give out a strong smell. The only way to manage this one is to be kind to yourself – if a certain food makes you feel sick, don't force yourself to eat it. You can find those nutrients in other foods. Have fun at the grocery store and pick out many different options for yourself. Once you're home, sort the ones that make you feel sick from the ones you can stand or actually like.

5. Food Cravings

And then you have the very opposite of food aversions – cravings! The feeling that you just gotta have it and you gotta have it *now*. For the most part, there's no harm in indulging your food cravings. However, it may become a problem if you're craving very specific foods all the time or your cravings are extremely unhealthy. Believe it or not, 30% of women report of craving non-food items such as soap or chalk. If you're experiencing non-food cravings, please do not satisfy these urges!

Before satisfying a craving, try drinking a tall glass of water first. It's actually surprisingly common to mistake thirst for hunger. Make sure you're not dehydrated before you rush to indulge. A second way to keep cravings at bay is by adding more protein to your diet. Studies have found a link between more protein at breakfast and the number of cravings throughout the day.

6. Frequent Urination

The need to frequently urinate can crop up as early as week 4 into your pregnancy – before you even know you're pregnant! Your kidneys need to become more efficient at getting rid of waste during your pregnancy, so this is an annoying side effect of extra blood flow going to your kidneys and pelvic area. Unfortunately, this symptom only becomes more extreme as pregnancy continues. Soon, your uterus will begin growing and so will your baby, increasing the amount of pressure on your bladder. There's no way to stop this altogether and it is highly advised that pregnant women do not minimize their water intake to attempt to control it. To avoid making it worse, limit your intake of coffee, tea, and soft drinks, which only increase the urgent need to urinate.

7. Tender and Swollen Breasts

Your body is preparing to provide nourishment to a baby and when the baby arrives, it'll need sustenance from your breasts. To prepare for this, your breasts will begin to grow and change – and this can result in skin that is tender or swollen. This starts in the first trimester and will continue throughout your entire pregnancy. If you're still using your pre-pregnancy bras, this may be exacerbating the issue. Give your breasts the support they need and consider purchasing a high-quality maternity bra. This may not solve the issue altogether but will definitely provide some relief.

8. Mood Swings

If you're feeling moody, restless, easily irritated, or just more down than usual, rest assured that it's completely normal. Depression and mood swings are common when your hormones are on overdrive. A key way to manage these symptoms is by making sure you're sleeping enough and eating a nutritious diet. Since your energy levels are already low, it's important you continue to recharge so your emotional wellbeing doesn't suffer. And always remember to make time for fun. If you're working while you're pregnant, make sure there's always time each day to devote to an activity that brings you joy.

9. Heartburn

During pregnancy, a woman produces higher levels of the hormone progesterone. This hormone has a soothing effect on certain muscles, including the ring of muscle in the esophagus. Unfortunately, when this muscle relaxes, it has a harder time keeping acids in your stomach, leading to acid reflux and – you guessed it – heartburn. To lower your chances of heartburn, doctors recommend avoiding spicy or acidic foods, eating smaller but more frequent meals, and waiting at least an hour before laying down after a meal. And to soothe heartburn, a glass of honey and milk or a small cup of yogurt can do wonders.

10. Skin Changes

You've likely heard of the 'pregnancy glow' where your cheeks get rosy and your entire complexion just seems a little brighter. Mothers-to-be tend to get the pregnancy glow in the first trimester, fairly early on. But unfortunately, not everyone will see positive changes. Some women will experience more oil than usual and this may even result in acne and breakouts. If you were prone to breakouts during your period, chances are that pregnancy will make you break out too. Thankfully, these skin changes are temporary and will subside once your hormones go back to normal. Whatever you do, steer clear of skin products with salicylic acid or vitamin A (retinol) unless you speak to a doctor first as these ingredients are known to affect pregnancy.

When to Call Your Doctor

You probably won't experience any big problems during your pregnancy, but it's always important to stay informed. If any of the following symptoms apply to you, call your doctor for additional help. It could indicate a more serious problem.

Heavy Vaginal Bleeding

Spotting is very common for pregnant women, but heavy bleeding is usually a cause for concern especially if there is any cramping or abdominal pain. In the early days, there is still a chance for a miscarriage or an ectopic pregnancy. Heavy bleeding can often be a signifier of one of these unfortunate complications.

Vaginal Discharge and Itching

It's completely normal to have some vaginal discharge during pregnancy – but look out for unusual discharge that's accompanied by itching. This could be a symptom of a sexually transmitted disease (STD). These are usually treatable but they can sometimes have negative effects on your pregnancy. If it's possible you have an STD, reach out to a doctor right away so it doesn't affect your baby.

Severe Nausea or Vomiting

Some level of morning sickness is an expected part of pregnancy, but if any of the following applies to you, contact your doctor.

- You vomit more than three times a day on most days.
- You've gone 12 hours without keeping down any liquid.
- You've thrown up blood, even if it's a small amount.

Urination with a Burning Sensation

Urinary Tract Infections (UTIs) are very common in pregnancy. While it's usually nothing to worry about, it becomes a more serious matter when you're pregnant. If left untreated, a UTI can cause a kidney infection, which has the potential to trigger a preterm birth or lead to a low birth-weight baby. Antibiotics from a doctor can easily solve the problem of a UTI, so it's essential mothers-to-be seek treatment for a fully preventable complication.

A High Fever

There are many potential causes for a high fever in pregnancy – while some of them are no cause for concern, it's important to rule out more serious causes. At its worst, it could be an infection, which may result in developmental complications in your growing baby. Even if you feel strongly that it's just a normal fever, doctors do not advise self-medicating since some pain-relieving medicines are dangerous during pregnancy. Be safe at any sign of a fever and call your doctor.

5 Ways Your Body Will Change in the First Trimester

As your body prepared to make a home for a baby, it will see a range of new changes and developments. While many of these will happen later on in the pregnancy, a good deal of changes will start as early as the first trimester.

1. Your Breasts

Pregnancy Guide

As your mammary glands increase in size, your breasts will swell to prepare for breastfeeding. Your areolas (the colored areas around your nipples) will also get darker and larger. For some women, the sweat glands in this area can also become larger, resulting in tiny, white bumps.

2. Vaginal Discharge

Pregnant women tend to get more vaginal discharge than they're used to. Normal discharge is milky with a thin consistency. Some women are more comfortable when they wear a small pad.

3. Hair Thickening

Many pregnant women report of thick and shiny hair that looks even healthier than it did before pregnancy. Unfortunately, this can also be accompanied by more hair growth on other areas of the body, such as the face, stomach, and sometimes even the back. You can thank rising estrogen levels for this!

4. Brittle Nails

Another side effect of higher estrogen levels is brittle nails. Many mothers find their nails are softer and more prone to splitting. It isn't all estrogen's fault, however; many experts think that increased blood flow in the toes and fingers could also be the culprit.

5. Bigger Feet

Don't worry, this doesn't happen to all women who get pregnant! Due to an increase in growth hormones, many mothers-to-be get bigger and sometimes flatter feet. It'll happen gradually over the course of your pregnancy. Believe it or not, some women have grown a whole shoe size!

What is a Doula & How Can They Help?

A birth doula is a trained professional whose primary job is to provide physical and emotional support to mothers over the course of their entire pregnancy. Although they can be hired at any time, including at the last minute, it's recommended that mothers hire a doula as early as possible, to allow more time for getting comfortable with your doula.

If you choose to hire a doula, she will assist you with the following:

- Breathing techniques, labor positions, and soothing through massage or other relaxation methods on the day of labor and delivery.
- Coaching and supporting the father (or other birth partner) so that they, too, can provide the best support for the new mother.
- Emotional support through the ups and downs of pregnancy, until the very end and perhaps even beyond.
- Letting you know whether you're in labor and when it's time to go to the hospital.
- Creating a more comforting environment for labor and delivery, e.g. with soft music, dim lights, candles, etc.
- Helping you to and from the bathroom (when needed) and making sure you've eaten and drunk enough on the day of delivery.

The contributions of a doula go far and wide, and many women claim they could never have done it without the help of one. This said, it's important to remember that a doula does not provide medical advice. Her assistance does not replace help from a doctor.

What Are the Benefits of Hiring a Doula?

Doulas have proven to have the following benefits on a mom and her pregnancy and childbirth experience:

- Significantly reduced anxiety.
- Decreases the time spent in labor by 25%.
- Less likely to need an epidural or other pain relief medication.
- Chances of needing a C-section lowered by 50%.
- Higher chances of breastfeeding success.
- A better bonding experience with the new baby.
- An overall more positive childbirth experience.

How Much Does a Doula Cost?

The cost of a doula varies widely and for some people, they may even be partially or completely covered by your health insurance provider. If you're paying out of pocket, expect a doula to cost between $800 and $2500.

Is a Doula Right for You?

As remarkable as a doula can be, not every mother feels she is the right fit for one – and that's totally okay! It all depends on your personality. Some women dislike the idea of someone they don't know being present during intimate moments. Keep in mind your doula will be there for some of your most difficult days. She will be getting up close and personal with you because that's the best way she can help. While most women find a doula's support empowering, others feel they get enough support from elsewhere.

If you have a very supportive and hands-on family with lots of pregnancy and childbirth experience, a doula may not be necessary. And if you take a long time to feel comfortable around a person you don't know well, your personality type may not be the right fit. But unless you fall into any of these categories, I've found that doulas are always incredible help. Many families stay in touch with their doulas because they gain a friend after the many months spent together. If you can afford it, consider a doula.

How Can I Find a Doula?

There are many ways to find the doula of your dreams. Try searching online directories such as:

- DONA International
- Birthing From Within
- Childbirth and Postpartum Professional Association (CAPPA)
- Doula Match

Choose the doula that suits your needs (in this case, you'd need a childbirth doula) and interview as many candidates as you can. You'll be spending a lot of time with this person so make sure that it's someone you feel comfortable with! And of course, always ensure that they have the right training and certifications. When you find the doula you're meant for, you'll get a good gut feeling!

For many moms, the first trimester is the most difficult – especially if you have some intense symptoms. Thankfully, some easier days are ahead. As moms transition into their next trimester, they find a lot of relief from their difficult symptoms.

Chapter 3 - The Second Trimester

Welcome to the second trimester! You're about halfway through the journey and you're probably incredibly relieved to reach this milestone. Many difficulties of the first trimester like morning sickness and fatigue will ease away in the second trimester. It's likely that you're feeling more energetic than you did and your breasts may even feel less tender. If you aren't feeling these positive developments yet, hold on! They'll get there soon enough.

In the first trimester, you will have gained little or no weight (unless you were very skinny) but this will change in the second trimester. Your belly will expand significantly in these next few months and you'll finally start to look pregnant. Since it's a period of rapid growth, this is when stretch marks are most likely to appear. You'll have more need for maternity clothes during this time, so make sure you're well-stocked with pregnancy wear that offers you comfort and support.

There's a lot happening inside your belly. Over the second trimester, these changes among many others begin to take effect:

- Your baby's organs are fully developed now.
- Your baby can hear! His or her first sounds will be the sound of your voice, the beating of your heart, the grumbling of your belly, and all the other fascinating noises of the human body.
- You'll finally be able to feel your baby moving around. This is more common later on in the second trimester.

Pelvic Floor Exercises that All Mothers Must Know

Now that you're more settled into your pregnancy, it's time to work on strengthening your pelvic floor muscles. This is a completely optional practice and will have no bearing whatsoever on your baby –

but mothers who strengthen their pelvic floor are always relieved they did. This practice is just for the benefit of mom!

During pregnancy and birth, a woman's pelvic floor is stretched beyond its usual limits. These muscles are responsible for keeping the bladder closed and controlling urine that goes out or stays in. When the pelvic floor muscles become weakened, a woman is more likely to leak urine accidentally, especially while sneezing, coughing, or straining in some way. Since these muscles also help keep the anus closed, there may even be less control over breaking wind.

Unfortunately, pelvic floor muscles do not get stronger on their own. To avoid the embarrassing moments listed, women must make the effort to strengthen their pelvic muscles and better yet, make these exercises part of their routine. Some of these exercises may feel difficult to do at first but with practice, you'll get the hang of them. Just as other muscles in your body can get stronger, so can your pelvic floor.

Isolating the Pelvic Floor Muscles

This is an essential first step and one that is best tried while sitting on the toilet. While urinating, stop the flow midstream. The muscles you've just activated are your pelvic floor muscles. See if you can stop yourself from urinating for two seconds and then continue emptying your bladder as normal. It's important to note that this is not a pelvic floor exercise; this is just a way to help beginners identify the pelvic floor muscles. It is not recommended to habitually stop urination midstream. If you find yourself tightening your buttocks while trying to isolate these muscles, then you haven't yet succeeded. It's okay – just keep trying!

Once you've identified your pelvic floor muscles, you're ready to start exercising them. If you're a beginner, it may be best to empty your bladder completely first. And a word of caution: stick to the reps listed and do not over-exercise – or you may find this practice backfiring.

- Exercise #1

This beginner's exercise can be performed anywhere, at any time. Tighten the muscles in your pelvic floor and hold them for ten seconds. Then, relax the muscles for ten seconds. Perform ten repetitions, three to five times a day.

- Exercise #2

Get into a sitting position and imagine that you're sitting on a marble. Next, tighten the muscles in your pelvic floor as if you're pulling that marble upwards. Imagine lifting the marble with your pelvic floor alone. Hold the marble for three seconds and then release it for three seconds. Perform ten to fifteen repetitions, three times a day.

- Exercise #3

Instead of holding the marble for three seconds, try only holding it for one second. To do this faster-paced exercise, pull the imaginary marble upwards quickly, lift it, and immediately release. Perform these fast contractions as well as the slower ones a few times a day.

5 Ways to Start Bonding With Your Baby

Although you can start bonding with your baby at any time, the second trimester is an especially wonderful time to do it. As I mentioned at the beginning of this chapter, your baby can now hear you. This opens up many more ways to bond with your little one. Here are some ways you can start bonding now:

1. Sing to Your Bump

Your baby knows your voice extremely well by now. Since its the main voice he or she hears, it has become a very soothing sound and vibration. Sing a song or melody you love and send that positivity inside your belly. Your baby will enjoy being soothed in this way.

2. Talk to Your Baby

If you're not much of a singer, then don't stress. Your baby likes your voice regardless of whether it's in tune or not. To bond through the sound of your voice, try talking directly to your baby instead. Tell him or her how excited you are to meet or what the best parts of your day were.

3. Respond to Kicks

This method of bonding can be very fun. The next time your baby kicks, rub or massage the spot where you felt the kick. Some mothers even find that the baby will kick again. A back-and-forth can ensue – almost like a conversation!

4. Self-Care

Taking care of your mind and body used to just mean taking care of *you*. With a baby on board, however, you're taking care of two people. During acts of self-care, you'll instantly feel more calm and at peace – and this means your baby will get the message too. The next time you take a warm bath or get massaged, both you and your baby can bond through the soothing and relaxing sensations.

5. Prenatal Yoga

Not only will prenatal yoga allow you to get good exercise, but it's also a great opportunity to feel close to your little bump. As you pay attention to your breath and keep an open awareness of the being inside you, your baby will instantly feel at peace. Overall, prenatal yoga has some very positive effects on a mother-to-be's wellbeing.

Watch Out For These Signs of Preeclampsia

During a woman's first pregnancy, her risk of developing preeclampsia is at its highest. This risk is raised even higher if she is obese, very young or older than 40, carrying more than one baby, conceived through in vitro fertilization or if she has a family history of preeclampsia

The major risk of preeclampsia is that it eventually leads to a life-threatening complication, such as organ damage, placental abruption or eclampsia – a very serious condition where both mom and baby are at risk of death. Unfortunately, the only way to cure preeclampsia is by delivering the baby and oftentimes, preeclampsia strikes when a baby is too young to be delivered. At this point, the new mother is left with a difficult decision: risk two lives and carry the baby to term or abort the pregnancy. Since preeclampsia can start as soon as 20 weeks into a pregnancy, it's important that you pay attention to your body's changes in the second trimester.

The symptoms of preeclampsia are:

- High blood pressure in pregnant women who have never before had high blood pressure.
- Sudden swelling in the face, eyes or hands – though keep in mind that ankle and feet swelling is completely normal during pregnancy.
- Rapid weight gain, especially over a few days.
- Severe headaches.
- Vision changes such as blurry vision, temporary loss of vision or sensitivity to light.
- Reduced urination or no urination at all.

- Excessive nausea and vomiting.
- Abdominal pain, especially if it occurs in the upper right side.
- Severe shortness of breath.

Your routine prenatal visits will keep track of potential preeclampsia signs. But since many of these symptoms can come on suddenly, it's essential that you seek help as soon as they arise. Do not take chances with preeclampsia symptoms.

The Best Ways to Exercise in the Second Trimester

You're starting to expand and you're likely wondering how you can get some safe exercise. The good news is that you can still do most of the activities you were doing in the first trimester. As long as exercise isn't strenuous and doesn't come with a fall risk, it's probably safe to do. Here are some of the most popular methods of exercise among pregnant women in the second trimester:

1. Swimming

No matter the trimester, whether it's the early days or late in the third trimester, swimming is one of the best ways for a pregnant woman to exercise. Not only is it incredibly safe (with absolutely zero fall-risk) and low-impact but many women find it soothing on their aches and pains. If you'd like to incorporate swimming into your exercise routine, just make sure to avoid strokes that require you to twist your middle-section and abdomen around. Go for 15-30 minute sessions (depending on how much you swam before you became pregnant) at least three times a week. If you're a more experienced swimmer, it is safe to do it daily.

2. Yoga

Pregnancy Guide

Remember when I said yoga is a great way to bond with your baby? It's also just a great form of exercise for all preggo moms. Yoga allows mom to breathe and stretch out her sore muscles, reducing the aches and pains of pregnancy. It can also teach her breathing techniques that may be beneficial later on during labor. To stay 100% safe, doctors advise sticking to gentle positions and avoiding poses like the Tree or Warrior which make it more possible for mom to fall over. And steer clear of poses that require you to lie on your back or twist at the waist. Hot yoga is also strongly discouraged during pregnancy.

3. Walking

Walking is always safe during pregnancy, so rest assured that if all other exercises fail, a good and leisurely walk will do the trick. Experts even recommend trying to engage the arms as you walk; this can build strength and flexibility in your upper body. For the best exercise, walk at a faster pace to get your heart rate a little higher. As long as you're free from a fall-risk (no difficult hiking!), this is completely safe for mom and baby. This is also true for women who are heavily pregnant.

4. Light Jogging

Light jogging and running are only recommended if you did this before you got pregnant. If you used to jog before, feel free to try a toned-down version of your previous routine. The most important thing is that you pay attention to your body and immediately stop running if you feel any back or joint pain. Fall-risk is also a concern with this exercise, so experts recommend only running on a treadmill with reliable safety features or a flat, unbroken sidewalk. Women who are not used to jogging or running are not advised to start doing it now.

10 Fun Ideas for the Second Trimester

If I had to choose the trimester I enjoy the most, it's by far the second trimester. With so many difficult pregnancy symptoms out of the way, you can finally embrace and enjoy being pregnant. No more nausea means food is wonderful again. No more fatigue means you can finally get some stuff done and feel good about it. You're at that perfect middle point. Here are some of my favorite fun second-trimester activities.

1. Have a Gender Reveal Party

Most women find out the gender of their baby in the second trimester. Know what this means? It's the perfect time for a gender reveal party! Gather your friends and family to celebrate the unveiling of your baby's gender. Many people enjoy filming the reactions of both parents to learning this exciting new detail about their baby. If you're interested in throwing a gender reveal party, there are a number of fun reveal ideas! Consider a gender reveal cake, balloon pop, confetti, or if you're feeling wild, fireworks!

2. Announce Your Pregnancy Publicly

Announcing a pregnancy in the first trimester is always risky since the chance of a miscarriage happening is highest at that point. Once you're in the second trimester, however, you can finally safely make the announcement! Whether you're holding a gender reveal party or not, you can have fun with your announcement to your wider group of friends on family. An adorable social media post or a beautiful card are some ideas you can use. What an exciting time!

3. Go on a Babymoon

Pregnancy Guide

If you've ever wanted a second honeymoon, now's your chance! The second trimester is a great time to enjoy your final vacation before having a kid. By the time the third trimester rolls around, you'll find that most airlines won't let you fly internationally, so now's the time to get your international travel fix. If you don't have the time or money for a big vacation, then why not see a different part of the country or have a staycation? Whatever form it takes, you and your partner should absolutely enjoy your last months as a child-free couple.

4. Go on a Shopping Spree for Maternity Clothes

You're going to see some significant weight gain in the second trimester and that means it's time for some new clothes. Go maternity shopping by yourself or with some other pregnant friends. And for the best selection, look online. Treat yourself to new clothes that make you feel fantastic about your new body. Many new moms prefer more fitted clothes to baggy clothes; this allows them to embrace their new curves, making them instantly feel more sexy. You deserve to feel good, first-time mom!

5. Buy Some Lingerie to Restart the Fire in the Bedroom

If you're feeling a little more sensual than usual, you can thank your fluctuating hormones! Enjoy these feelings and bring your partner into the mix to enjoy them too. If you're so inclined, throw in some new lingerie the next time you go maternity clothes shopping. You'll get a lot bigger in the third trimester so now's the time to get lingerie you can still wear after you're pregnant!

6. Have a Maternity Photoshoot

Flaunt your new body and feel beautiful! Maternity photoshoots are not about vanity; it's about commemorating a beautiful time in your life. As a first-time mom, how wonderful would it be to make memories if your experience in the form of gorgeous photographs? The second trimester is perfect as you look pregnant enough for a maternity shoot but you're not big enough to start getting self-conscious. Browse online for a good maternity photographer or ask for referrals from friends. It may sound like a wild idea but many mothers deeply cherish these photos! Feel free to get your partner involved as well.

7. Incorporate Gentle Exercise into your Routine

Now that you're in the second trimester, you've likely gotten your energy back. Without the fatigue to hold you back, it's a great time to start getting into gentle exercise. Take a look at the previous section and find an exercise method that you like best! If you weren't very fit before you got pregnant, take it easy as you're not any fitter now that you're expecting. Always listen to your body!

8. Decorate and Furnish the Nursery

When your baby arrives, you'll want to have the nursery completely ready. If you're planning on having it painted, it's especially important that there aren't any lingering paint fumes. Get the essentials out of the way in the second trimester while you have the energy to decorate and furnish. The bigger you get, the less time you're going to want to spend on your feet. If paint and chemicals need to be handled, get your partner to take over this job and make sure you aren't inhaling any dangerous fumes.

9. Interview More Doulas

If you haven't decided on a doula or are making last minute decisions about having one, now's the time to get serious about the search. Doulas can be hired at any time but the earlier you have one on board, the more help they can offer. Interview more doula candidates and have one decided on before your second trimester ends. It's totally possible to have fun with this! Many doulas end up forming a friendship with the family, so you can even try to see this as interviewing a potential new family friend. Get to know these candidates and laugh with them. If you're still struggling to find a childbirth doula, search for them online or ask other mothers you know for referrals.

10. Take a Childbirth Class

It's not too late to take a childbirth class. If you didn't attend one in your first trimester, consider doing it now. Mothers who make the time to take these classes are always glad they did – and some birthing centers even require you to take them! The information you'll glean is invaluable. Another bonus? You'll meet other first-time moms, the perfect allies on this crazy ride! Connecting with other first-time moms is one of the best things you can do for yourself. When both your babies are born, you can empower each other and help each other learn. When you're done with childbirth class, consider taking others on breastfeeding or newborn care.

Chapter 4 - The Third Trimester

You're finally in the home stretch of your pregnancy the third and last trimester. This trimester is easily the most exciting as it ends with the ultimate reward: bringing your baby out into the world and getting to hold him or her in your arms. Keep in mind that, although you may have a due date set, there's a chance your baby will arrive sooner than you expect. It's important that you recognize the signs you're going into labor, as soon as they arise. But before we get into that, here's a quick rundown on how your baby is continuing to develop in these final months:

- Your baby's eyelashes have formed and he or she is now capable of opening their eyelids.
- It's finally happened! Your baby can kick! He or she can also stretch and gently grasp.
- Hair has grown – and if you have thick hair genes, it's possible your baby is starting to develop a fantastic head of hair.
- What a little cutie – your baby's skin is now smooth and taking on a chubby appearance.

To sum up, your baby is finally starting to resemble a full-on tiny human. Your body is putting the finishing touches on the child you'll soon hold in your arms. In the meantime, however, there's a lot to do to prepare for his or her arrival.

Every First-Time Mom's To-Do List for the Third Trimester

1. Finish Your Baby's Nursery

Pregnancy Guide

As soon as your little bundle comes home from the hospital, you'll want to have his or her nursery ready to be slept in. This means you'll need a cot. If you plan on painting the nursery, get this done as soon as possible so that your baby does not have to be exposed to the smell of paint – which can be harmful if exposure lasts for more than a brief moment.

2. Prepare Everything Your Baby Will Need

When your baby comes, the last thing you'll want to do is rush to the store. Both you and your partner will want to enjoy every second of being with your newborn – any interruption would be extremely annoying! The third trimester is the perfect time to stock up on your baby's essentials so you don't need to run out for them later. You'll need diapers, blankets, newborn onesies, and much more. Get the full list in the following chapter.

3. Read as Much as You Can

This new chapter of your life is like no other chapter you've known before. This is why it's strongly encouraged for all mothers to fully inform themselves about how to properly care for a child. Thankfully for all mothers, there's a lot of information out there, easily accessible to all. In fact, by reading this book, you're already making strides towards being a fully prepared mom! Still, you shouldn't stop at one book. Absorb as much information as you can from as many sources as possible.

4. Make Self-Care a Priority

You're carrying a child and your body deserves all the love it can get. Do everything you can to avoid strain and needless stress. Actively practice self-care. Pamper yourself with a prenatal massage at a great spa and when you're feeling tired, sit in bed and enjoy your favorite

TV show. Do whatever makes you feel great. And keep in mind that self-care sometimes means doing something that is good for you, even if you don't really feel like doing it. Sure, treat yourself to a chocolate milkshake if it brings you joy, but more often than not, care for yourself by seeking out more nutritious options. To operate from a mindset of self-care, consider what your body really needs at that moment to create the best emotional environment for your baby.

5. Start a Baby Registry

There's no reason you should buy all the essentials yourself! Baby registries allow parents-to-be to list all items they need when their baby arrives. This, then, allows friends and family to give these items as gifts. Consider making your own baby registry on Amazon, Bed Bath & Beyond or Target.

6. Stock Your Freezer

With a new baby around, new parents tend to have a lot less energy for their regular cook-ups. Still, that's no excuse to neglect your hungry bellies and nutrient intake. You're going to need those calories! The third trimester is the perfect time to stock your freezer with microwavable meals or anything that doesn't require more than two steps to prepare. Pack as much in as you can. Neither you nor your partner will want to head out to the grocery store with a new little baby. If you prefer home-cooked meals, then an alternative is to cook your own meals to freeze for later.

7. Clean the House

This may seem like a strange to-do activity, but trust me, you'll be glad you did it when your baby comes. A surprising number of moms wish they'd cleaned up their home before their baby's arrival. Once the little bundle comes, there's simply no time or energy to deal with a messy house. Whether you do it with a partner or hire someone else to do it, try and get your home spic-and-span and mess-free before your big day.

8. Rest!

Once mothers enter the third trimester, it gets a little more difficult to sleep. No matter what you do, you just can't seem to get as comfortable as you used to. Nevertheless, it's important that moms get as much rest as they can. With childbirth on the horizon and exhausting days with a newborn baby looming, now's the time to try and get some much needed rest. It won't just be you and your partner for long! Make the most of the time you have to stay horizontal for as long as you like.

9. Decide Whether to Breast or Bottle-feed

To breastfeed or formula-feed – that is the question. Or at least, it is *one of* the questions of the third trimester. If you haven't decided yet, it's about time you do so. Why? Because very soon you'll need to start shopping to prepare for your new baby. And breastfeeding and bottle-feeding moms need slightly different equipment. If you're still feeling indecisive, let's examine the advantages of both options.

Breastfeeding vs. Formula Feeding

Breast

- When it comes to the nutrition factor, breast really is best. Mothers pass antibodies through their breast milk, meaning that their child is more resistant to certain illnesses and infections, such as meningitis and ear infections.
- Breast milk is easier to digest than other options. This means there's a much lower chance of your baby getting gassy or constipated.

- Breastfeeding is the least expensive option. You will need to buy formula but breast milk is, as you know, completely free. The money you spend on formula will quickly add up but breastfed babies just not you, a breast pump, bottles, and very few other supplies.
- Studies have shown there is some link between breastfeeding and babies with high levels of intelligence, i.e. cognitive function.
- Breastfeeding is also great for mothers. There is evidence that breastfeeding mothers have a lower risk of getting breast cancer, diabetes, ovarian cancer and more.
- Experts aren't so sure why but there appears to be a connection between breastfed babies and a reduced risk for Sudden Infant Death Syndrome (SIDS). Babies who are breastfed for at least six months are much less likely to die in their sleep.
- When breastfeeding happens regularly, it can burn up to 500 calories per day. If you're interested in shedding weight quickly after pregnancy, breastfeeding can help greatly.

Formula

- Formula feeding is far more convenient for mothers. Formula can be fed at any time and there is no need to take time out of your schedule to pump milk. This means your partner can feed the baby at any time, without needing help from you first.
- Babies don't digest formula as quickly as they digest breast milk, so there will be far more time between formula-feeds as opposed to breastfeeds. In other words, your baby will not need to be fed as often.
- There's no need to restrict your diet in any way. Babies that consume breast milk are very affected by what their mother eats and drinks, but with a formula-fed baby, mom can have

whatever she likes. Foods and drinks that mothers should avoid while breastfeeding include hot spices, citrus fruits, alcohol, and anything with a high amount of caffeine. For the full list, see Chapter 8.

Tackling Third-Trimester Insomnia

As I mentioned previously, insomnia in the third trimester is not uncommon, especially for first-time moms. A number of factors contribute to this inability to sleep, from frequent urination and body pains to simply feeling huge and not being able to get comfortable. All new moms need their precious sleep; here are some helpful tips for fighting pregnancy insomnia.

1. **Invest in a high-quality pregnancy pillow.** You can find these in most maternity stores and they will work wonders for your sleep routine. Pregnancy pillows provide the perfect amount of support for mom so she can finally get in a comfortable position. Doctors actually recommend that pregnant women sleep on their left side after week 20, as this allows more blood flow to get to your baby. A pregnancy pillow is designed to make this position more comfortable.
2. **Make light exercise part of your routine.** As much as moms hate to hear it at this point in their pregnancy, a little daily exercise can help greatly. It may be difficult but try to get up and about at least once a day – it'll make you sleepier at night. Just try not to do it too close to your bedtime or you'll be buzzing with energy.
3. **Wear loose and comfortable nightwear.** Steer clear of tight-fitting clothing and stick to light materials like cotton that allow your body to breathe. And if sleeping in the nude is the most comfortable for you, then why not? Do whatever you need to get sleep, first-time mom.

4. **Use as many pillows as you need.** This is especially important if you can't afford a pregnancy pillow. Get all the cushions and pillows in your home together (though you should probably leave at least one for your partner!) and experiment with as many arrangements and configurations as you can. Remember that sleeping on your left side is best for your baby right now. To mimic the support of a pregnancy pillow, try putting a cushion under your belly and between your knees.
5. **Sleep wherever you get comfortable.** If it's on your living room sofa or in an armchair, go for it. It doesn't have to be in your bed. Wherever you find yourself drifting off, allow yourself to just fall asleep. Sleep is hard to come by so take it whenever it comes.
6. **Fully hydrate by the early evening.** This way, you'll cut down on the number of times you need to go to the bathroom in the middle of the night and you'll still get all the water you need. Start hydrating as soon as you get up and stop drinking water when the evening rolls in.
7. **Get help from your doctor.** Thing is, some sleep medications and aids are perfectly fine to have while pregnant – but you should never go on them without telling your doctor first. If no other methods work, feel free to ask your doctor for more serious relief. He or she will be able to prescribe a sleep aid that is safe for your baby and exactly what you need.

Labor Signals & What They Mean

Natural birth or C-section, it's vital that every mother-to-be recognizes when they're going into labor. Even if your due date isn't for a few more weeks, it's always possible to have a premature baby. Each mother is going to have a slightly different experience during the weeks or days before labor sets in, but here are some of the many signals you're likely to experience and what they mean.

- Your Baby Has 'Dropped'

When the baby starts to sink lower into the pelvis, this is a key sign that the body is preparing for labor. But hold up, this doesn't necessarily mean that you're on the verge. A baby drop can happen as early as a month before labor.

- An Increase in Back Pain and Cramping

As your body prepared for birth, your joints and muscles with shift around and stretch. Unfortunately, this means more back pain and cramping for mom. While this is certainly a sign that labor is coming somewhat soon, there is no need to rush to the hospital. This signal means labor is as far as a month away and soon as a few days away.

- Bloody Show

In late pregnancy, thick vaginal discharge mixed with mucus and blood gets released by the vagina. This pink-hued discharge is called the 'bloody show' and it's a sign that the cervix is preparing for labor. The bloody show can indicate that labor is anywhere from a few weeks to a few hours away. If it's accompanied by other signals on this last, then labor may be close.

- Your Water Breaks

The water break is one of the last signs of labor a woman will experience. In other words, if it happens to you, you're most certainly in labor and your baby is on the way soon. Movies have misled people into thinking a public water break is common – but in reality, a premature break rarely happens. For most women, the water break happens well into labor and sometimes even moments before the baby actually emerges.

- Contractions

During labor, intense contractions are known to precede the time of delivery, but false-alarm contractions do exist. And this can confuse matters for many women. Braxton Hicks contractions are not labor contractions. Instead, they signal that the body is getting ready or warming up. There are many ways to tell Braxton Hicks contractions from Labor contractions, the most notable difference being that real contractions get more intense and closer together. When this is felt, you're most definitely in labor!

Braxton Hicks Contractions vs. Labor Contractions

Even though we've covered one way to distinguish between a false-alarm and real labor contraction, there are other signifiers too. No one wants to drag themselves all the way to the hospital just to be told to go home again – so let's make sure you understand these key differences! Here's how to know whether you're truly in labor or not:

Intensity

Braxton Hicks - These contractions are usually mild in intensity, without much variation in strength. Many women have also experienced them as strong to start with but weaker over time.

Labor - Contractions that indicate real labor have nowhere to go but up in intensity. They only get stronger and stronger over time.

Pain

Braxton Hicks - Pain is located on the front of your body, in your lower abdomen.

Labor - Pain exists in both the abdomen and the back. Some women even report that pain is *more* extreme in the back of the body. This is because the whole body prepares for real labor, not just one side.

Timing

Braxton Hicks - There is no discernible pattern between contractions. They come on seemingly at random with no specific regularity. They do not become more frequent.

Labor - Contractions come regularly and get closer together.

Adjustments

Braxton Hicks - Contractions stop or weaken with a change of position such as sitting, laying down, or walking.

Labor - It doesn't matter what you do, labor contractions still continue.

How Do You Induce Labor Safely and Naturally?

For labor to happen, two hormones are needed – prostaglandins and oxytocin. These two hormones trigger contractions and help to expand the cervix so that a baby can emerge. The key to inducing labor mostly revolves around trying to stimulate these hormones and therefore, labor. While many 'old wives tales' exist around the use of certain herbs, studies have not yet been performed to prove their efficiency or safety. Furthermore, many people suggest castor oil as a way to induce labor. I can confirm this method *does work*, but I highly discourage using it as it is also a laxative. Mothers who use castor oil end up going into labor dehydrated and with diarrhea. Do not make labor harder on yourself!

It is also extremely important to note that no one should try to induce labor unless they are due or past their due date. Inducing labor before your time should not be done unless a doctor gives you the OK.

- Nipple Stimulation

Let's make one thing clear: this type of nipple stimulation is not sexual at all! For this method to be successful, stimulation needs to mimic the suckling of a baby. Doing this will release oxytocin in the brain and may result in your uterus contracting, therefore beginning the process of labor.

- Membrane Sweeping or Stripping

If you're desperate, membrane sweeping is always an option – though it must be performed by your doctor. Using a gloved finger, your doctor will reach inside you to separate the amniotic sac from an area just inside the cervix. This releases prostaglandins and stimulates contractions to induce labor. Expect some discomfort during this procedure.

- Having Sex

It's important to note that sex doesn't always work at inducing labor. Still, there's a chance it might. Not only does sex release prostaglandins but male ejaculate also contains it. If the man ejaculates inside the vagina, it's possible the cervix will wake up and start contracting.

- Eating Dates

This method will not induce labor instantly, but if you start a few weeks before pregnancy, you may never have to induce labor. Studies have shown that eating 60-80 grams of dates per day in late pregnancy can reduce the need for induction and improve labor overall. Women who ate dates regularly decreased the length of the first stage of labor to almost half the time of women who didn't.

Chapter 5 - Preparing for the Big Day

When the big day arrives, the last thing you want to be is unprepared. No matter the type of birth you're having, there are a variety of ways you can and should make yourself more comfortable. Just a little prep can go a long way. Unprepared first-time mothers find themselves far more stressed and uncomfortable when the big moment arises – so avoid this, now that you have the choice. Follow these simple steps and you'll have everything you need to devote your full attention to you and your baby.

Pack These 13 Essentials in Your Hospital Bag

There's a possibility your little one will come knocking sooner than you think – so start packing your hospital bag just in case! Mothers who pack at the last minute (or allow someone to do it for them!) have admitted to ending up with a lot of useless stuff they didn't really need and without the stuff they really *did* need. The birth of your first child will be such a special time and the last thing you want is to be inconvenienced by something you could have prepared for.

1. Your Daily Toiletries

What essential toiletries are part of your morning and nighttime routine? Pack travel-sized versions in your bag. A stay at the hospital is no reason to neglect your self-care; in fact, it's a bigger reason to make it a priority. Bring your toothbrush, toothpaste, deodorant, and whatever else makes you feel cozy and at home. For efficiency and ease, consider getting some cleansing facial wipes instead of your usual face wash.

2. Hair Ties and Clips

Pregnancy Guide

The last thing you want is your hair getting in your face while you're giving birth. Pack hair ties and/or clips to keep your hair pulled back so you can focus on the big task without any minor annoyances.

3. Snacks and Drinks

This one is easily overlooked. It's not that food and drink aren't available where you'll be, it's more about the fact that mom and dad often want to stay together. Swept up in the special moment, it isn't uncommon for dad to opt for staying with mom instead of going off wandering for food. Without snacks readily available, many new parents can forget it's been several hours since their last meal.

4. Lip Balm

Have something that keeps your lips moisturized. Many mothers find their lips get chapped as they endure the intense hard work of labor. Keep those lips hydrated!

5. Comfortable Shoes

Ideally, these should be easy to slip on and off as you may want to do some walking around the hospital. Avoid all shoes that require you to bend over and/or strain in any way to get them on.

6. Pillows

Every hospital will provide pillows but don't expect them to be as comfortable as the ones you have at home. To ensure you're as comfortable as possible during this special but physically challenging time, bring your favorite pillow from home. Your partner may also want to bring a pillow as well.

7. A Dark-Colored Bathrobe or Dressing Gown

Whether it's in early labor or the postnatal ward, you're definitely going to be up and about in the hospital at some point. Make sure you're warm and comfortable by bringing something to wear over your hospital clothes. If you're worried about stains showing, pack something that's dark-colored.

8. Entertainment

Since mom will be preoccupied most of the time, this is more of a 'need' for dad. Pack something that can provide entertainment for many hours. This could be a book, a magazine, a music player, or something else. Whatever it is, make sure that it doesn't stress out or overwhelm mom!

9. Loose Clothes

Bring comfortable clothes, not just for the hospital but for your first ride home with your baby. It's important that you're not wearing anything too tight as you'll feel tender after delivery. Pack clothes that open easily at the front. This way, you'll be able to feed your baby with no difficulty as soon as the need arises.

10. Postpartum Underwear

Many first time moms get the mistaken impression that the hospital will supply them with proper underwear. Those who don't get *that* mistaken impression instead wrongly assume that it's fine to bring the underwear they wear normally. For starters, do *not* bring underwear that you would be upset to ruin. You will bleed heavily after giving birth and you'll need something that is up to the task. Get high-quality postpartum underwear that provides support, protection, and comfort.

11. Eyeglasses

This only applies to you if you wear them, of course. New mothers tend to not want to deal with their contact lenses when they're giving birth at a hospital. Since labor can take a while and it's possible you may be in and out of sleep, glasses tend to be the easier option. This may be down to personal preference. But if you're having a C-section, keep in mind you will be asked to remove your contact lenses beforehand.

12. Everything You Need to Be Photo-Ready

For some moms, this may mean nothing at all – but others might like to bring some mascara or powder to look a little less worn out in photos. This is completely up to mom and her preferences. Your partner and family members are likely excited to document the special day so bring any clothes or makeup you need to feel wonderful.

13. Massage Oil or Lotion

During the hours before labor or even after birth, many moms find massage incredibly soothing. Kick this up a notch by bringing a massage oil or lotion with a fragrance you find pleasant.

22 New-Baby & First-Time Mom Necessities

Of course, preparation is not just about the hospital visit and childbirth. It's also about that other special day – the day you get to bring your little one home. As soon as you get home, you'll need to have everything ready. Aside from a fully finished nursery with a crib or bassinet, you'll also need your child's smaller necessities. Take note of the following essentials; if you don't get them through your baby registry, get them yourself as soon as you can.

1. Diapers

Your newborn is gonna be one heck of a pooper – there's no way to avoid it! Needless to say, you're going to need diapers and a lot of them. Every mom can take their pick of disposable or cloth diapers.

- Disposable

Pros: Most convenient option, more absorbent, less time-consuming.

Disposable diapers are still a wildly popular option and it's no wonder why. The toss-when-you're-done approach is very convenient and requires no extra cleaning from mom or dad. But be prepared to spend more money in the long run – on average, parents who use disposables spend upwards of $2000 over two years. Not only this but the total amount of diapers used will create a lot of non-biodegradable waste for the environment. If you prefer the ease of disposable diapers, consider getting eco-friendly products from companies like *Honest*.

- Cloth

Pros: Much cheaper in the long run, adjustable, kinder to sensitive skin, irritation less likely, reusable, eco-friendly.

Over recent years, cloth diapers have become more widely used. Not only is it a money-saving option but cloth diapers today are far more effective than they used to be, thanks to innovation around eco-friendly baby products. To safeguard against potential skin irritation, cloth diapers are the way to go since absorbent chemicals in disposables can cause bad skin reactions for some babies. However, all parents who choose this route should keep in mind that cloth diapers require a lot more effort and time. Once your batch of diapers has been soiled, they'll need to be deep cleaned.

2. One-Piece Baby Clothes

Save the cute two-pieces for when your baby is a tiny bit older. To start off, focus on onesies or one-piece clothing that is easy to put on and take off. Since babies are extremely messy, you'll need to change your baby's clothes many times a day – keep this in mind when choosing clothes! Ideally, these garments should snap open at the bottom so you can do a diaper change with minimal hassle.

3. Mittens

If the onesies you've purchased don't cover your newborns hands, then some mittens will serve your newborn well. These are to ensure they don't scratch themselves with their little nails. Just two pairs should do the trick.

4. Baby Wipes

Try to get baby wipes that are suitable for more sensitive skin. Although your baby may not need a sensitive solution, it is always best to be safe with a newborn. These wipes will be used to clean your baby's bottom half during changing. On these sensitive areas, more care is needed.

5. Receiving Blankets

These multi-purpose blankets can be used for a myriad of things and they'll be your best friends in the months to come. Receiving blankets are soft, made of thin cotton, and usually come in a pack of three or four. Not only will these blankets provide your baby with comfort and warmth, but they also make great burping cloths, playmats, and feeding blankets for if you want more privacy during public breastfeedings.

6. Burp Cloths

As the name suggests, burp cloths are for covering clothes and wiping up spills, in the event that your baby spits up. And believe me, it will happen a lot. Receiving blankets can make handy substitute burp cloths but traditional burp cloths are much smaller and easier to carry around. While that extra surface area can be nice, it's not always entirely necessary.

7. Swaddling Blankets

To keep your baby comfortable and fully supported, you'll want to tuck him or her into a swaddling blanket. Again, a receiving cloth can be used as one, but real swaddling blankets are larger in size, more stretchy, and oftentimes, specially designed so that mom and dad can swaddle their baby with minimal hassle.

8. A Baby Carrier

You're going to need an easy, comfortable way to carry your baby around with you. This is where a baby carrier comes in. This way, your little one can snuggle in close while you get around to do what you need to do. A good carrier offers your baby secure, safe and comfortable support. In the early days, a baby carrier is the best way to travel with your baby as it promotes intimacy and skin-to-skin contact. If you have a big baby or suffer from back problems, you may find a carrier uncomfortable – in which case you may need to pass on carrier duties to your partner.

9. Baby Bottles with Nipples

You'll need baby bottles whether you're breastfeeding or bottle-feeding. If you're feeding your baby breastmilk, you'll still need a way to feed your baby expressed milk so he or she can be fed without you around. These days, most parents prefer to use glass bottles to avoid the chemicals in plastic passing into the milk.

10. Changing Pad

Most parents designate an area in the room to change their baby's diaper. This changing station is usually made up of a changing pad on a solid, sturdy surface. Keep in mind that you'll be using this station multiple times a day, so it's important that it isn't wobbly, is in an area that gets enough light, and doesn't require mom or dad to crouch over in an uncomfortable position. Some parents also like to have a back-up changing pad in case the main one gets soiled.

11. A Diaper Genie or Pail

You're going to need a proper place to store dirty diapers between trash runs. Regular trash cans don't always do a great job at masking the bad odors – and this is where a diaper genie comes in. A genie or pail is capable of storing a load of dirty diapers without letting the bad smells waft into the room. If you have a big house, a diaper genie may not be absolutely necessary, but if your home is a tighter fit, you're going to want to keep that diaper smell out of the other rooms.

12. Car Seat

You're going to need a car seat as soon as you get into the car with your baby to head home from the hospital. For a newborn baby, it is advised that you purchase a rear-facing car seat. Until the age of two years-old, your baby should *not* use a forward-facing car seat.

13. Stroller

While a baby carrier pretty much always suffices for taking your baby wherever you need to go, you're eventually going to crave the freedom of a stroller – especially for taking your baby outdoors. And once your baby starts getting heavy, a stroller becomes an absolute must-have. Unlike a carrier, a stroller allows a baby to lay flat on his or her back and sleep comfortably. And once your baby ages, they can easily interact with the world while remaining comfortable. One of the other great things about a stroller is that it also gives mom a place to store baby essentials while on-the-go.

14. A Baby Bathtub

Many mothers survive just fine without a baby bathtub, but they make things a lot more convenient when bathing your baby. These days, baby bathtubs come with all kinds of hi-tech features, including temperature indicators. Feel free to purchase whatever makes the most sense for your budget. The most essential feature is the space it provides for your newborn to get wet, but not too submerged. Moms who opt out of the baby bathtub choose to just get in the big bathtub with their newborn in their lap. Or another alternative, using the sink. If you don't have a lot of space in your home, these two alternatives may be the best choice. Whatever you do – baby bathtub or not – do not get a bathtub ring as these pose more dangers than they prevent.

15. A Nursing Bra

When your milk comes in, your breasts are going to get much bigger. This means none of your current bras are going to be very helpful – including your pregnancy bras. To ensure you get the most comfort and support for your breasts, get fitted for a nursing bra. Ideally, you should do this as close to your expected due date as possible and no earlier than a month before. You are unlikely to be in the mood after your baby comes, so doing this beforehand is best.

For Breastfeeding

16. A Breast Pump

If you plan on breastfeeding, a breast pump is a core necessity. This allows you to express and store milk in advance so your baby can be fed even if you're asleep or away. If you find yourself engorged or with an oversupply of milk, a breast pump will be your best friend.

17. Containers or Bags for Milk Storage

After expressing milk, you're going to need a place to store it until it's needed. Ideally, it should be in something that is designed to store breast milk. There are many options for this and it all comes down to personal preference. Moms can take their pick of glass containers, breast milk trays, storage bags, or plastic milk bottles.

18. Nipple Cream or Lanolin Ointment

Believe me, your nipples are going to get sore. While there's no sure way to prevent it entirely if you're breastfeeding, you can take measures to avoid cracked and dry nipples. Applying cream or ointment to your nipples everyday can work wonders.

19. Breast Pads

When breastfeeding a baby, it isn't uncommon for the other breast (the one that's not feeding your baby) to also let out milk. As you'd expect, this can lead to a little and sometimes a lot of leaking. Some moms naturally leak more than others and it may have to do with their supply. Even when you're not breastfeeding, you'll likely experience leaking, especially once your baby starts sleeping longer hours and your body hasn't adjusted to the new schedule. And this is where breast or nursing pads come in to save the day. They prevent milk from leaking through your clothes. Mothers that don't intend to breastfeed also find breast pads helpful sometimes, as it's possible to experience some leaking before milk production dries up.

For Formula Feeding:

20. Formula

This one is a given! If you plan on formula-feeding your baby, make sure you have a large stock of all the formula you need for the next few to several weeks. It's important that the formula you buy is suitable for your newborn. The three types of formula are ready-to-use, powdered, or concentrated liquid. Talk to your doctor to determine the right kind of formula for your baby.

For Postpartum Healing

21. Maxi Pads

If you're planning on a vaginal birth, stock up on some maxi pads. You're going to be bleeding a lot after giving birth; make sure you're underwear and clothing are fully protected with these new mom essentials. You'll be using these for several weeks after giving birth and believe me, tampons will not do. If you're a waste-conscious person and you'd prefer to not use disposable products, know that there are plenty of reusable cloth maxi pads as well. Many moms find these even more comfortable than disposable pads.

22. A Tummy Splint

After pregnancy, many women experience abdominal separation. This is when the left and right stomach muscles separate slightly, resulting in tummy fat that looks disjointed from the rest of the stomach. This isn't just an aesthetic concern, it can also cause constipation, lower back pain, and at its most extreme, a hernia.

Abdominal separation is very common and happens to about two-thirds of pregnant women. Unfortunately, sit-ups can make the issue worse and while time can heal most of the problem, many moms are still left with a little pooch. The tummy splint is the easiest and safest way to minimize the problem after birth. This compression wrap applies light pressure so that mom's body has support and just the right amount of 'push' inwards. Even if abdominal separation isn't a huge concern for you, many moms find a compression wrap very comforting.

How to Start Creating a Birth Plan

On the day of your child's birth, you're probably not going to feel like making any big decisions. This is where the birth plan comes in. Having a birth plan prepared means your decisions and wishes about your baby's delivery are documented ahead of time. When your baby comes knocking, this means all your preferences are clearly outlined – so you can just focus on birthing your little bundle.

Keep in mind that sometimes unpredictable circumstances strike during birth, so there's always a possibility doctors will insist on a different course of action. And you, yourself, may want to make these changes. In any case, it is always helpful to create a birth plan. This step is completely optional, but many moms like having the chance to discuss and think through these decisions ahead of time. This is what you should include in your birth plan:

- List the basics

These include your name, contact information, and your doctor's name. If you know which hospital you'll be delivering at, include the name of this hospital too.

- Name all attendants

Who of your friends and family would you like to be present in the delivery room? Having this in your birth plan will ensure they're all allowed in during your big moment.

- Atmosphere preferences

Pregnancy Guide

Think of the environment that you'd most like to give birth in. What do you find calming or soothing? Would you like the lights dimmed or any type of music playing in the background? Are there any items from home that you need beside you to give you strength?

- Your labor preferences

Would you like to be photographed or filmed? Would you like to walk around freely? Birthing equipment may be available, such as a birthing stool or chair; include whether you would like anything like this. If you like the idea of being in a tub for labor and delivery, include this in your plan as well. And if you'd prefer to opt out of an episiotomy (snipping of the perineum for easier delivery), say so and be prepared to discuss this with your doctor.

- Pain management preferences

When the intensity of labor sets in, what are your preferences around the use of an epidural? What about other pain medications? If you're fine with the use of an epidural or other pain relief, would you like it as soon as possible or would you like to wait and see if you can do without it first? If you don't want any of the above pain medications, are there any alternatives you'd prefer?

- Delivery preferences

Would you like the opportunity to watch your baby emerge with a mirror? Many mothers even want to touch their baby's head as it crowns. If you have preferences around whether to have an episiotomy when necessary or to allow natural tearing, mention this. When your baby is out, would you like the father to cut the umbilical cord? If you're having a C-section, would you like the drape removed so you can watch your baby being lifted out of you? Do you want everyone else in the room to be silent so that your voice is the first thing your baby hears? It's possible that you may also have an IV or catheter inserted, so if you want to steer clear of this, include this.

For clarity's sake, it's always best if the birth plan is less than a page long and easy to read. Once you're done, share your birth plan with your partner and your doctor. Their input may be helpful before the plan is finalized.

Chapter 6 - Childbirth & Labor

At last, the time has come! The big day has arrived and everything you've prepared for in your childbirth class stands before you. Hopefully, your hospital bag is fully packed by now – if it isn't, get your partner or family member to gather what you'll need most (pillows, hair ties, and snacks!) and accept they may need to come back later. If it's your first birth, you're likely having it at the hospital either via planned or unplanned C-section, or natural birth. If you have a doula and she's not yet with you, it's time to let her know that your time is finally here.

By now, you, your partner, your doctor, and your doula (if you have one) should be well aware of the decisions laid out in your birth plan. Everyone will be trying their best to honor your wishes, but stay flexible. Unexpected things can happen which makes it difficult to honor very specific preferences; just know that whatever course of action is made, it will be in the best interest of you and your baby.

When it comes to childbirth, a good rule of thumb is to always expect the unexpected. No two births are exactly the same, even from the same mother. This said, there are many things to keep in mind on this big day. It's possible that not all of it will apply to you, but it's always helpful to prepare for the unexpected the best you can.

10 Less-Known Things You Should Know About Vaginal Childbirth & Labor

Everyone knows vaginal childbirth is challenging and painful, but what else? So much happens during labor – stuff you'd never know about unless you'd gone through it! – and all pregnant women should have the complete picture.

1. **Your doctor may not be with you until the very end, and sometimes, not even then.** Despite your many doctor visits, he or she won't really be needed until delivery takes place. Since midwives and other professionals are fully equipped and skilled to handle labor, there's no need for the doctor during this part of the process. The doctor may slip in and out to check in on you, but do not expect more attention than that. It's also possible that your doctor won't even deliver your baby, especially if he or she has partners at the facility.
2. **It's possible you'll get sent home, even if your contractions are real labor contractions.** Even though contractions definitely signify that you're in labor, the reality is that labor can last days. Unless your contractions are very frequent, coming every five minutes or less, then there's a possibility you'll get turned away at the hospital and told to come back later.
3. **The pain might be far more tolerable than you think - or far worse.** There's absolutely no way to predict how painful your childbirth will be. Of course, all women should expect some pain, but I've known many women who were blessed with relatively easy labors and a baby out in under ten minutes. On the other hand, I've also known women who claimed childbirth was even worse than they thought. There's no sure way to know.
4. **You will probably poop in the middle of childbirth.** Many women are horrified to learn this fact, but unfortunately there's no way to ensure it doesn't happen. The reason behind this is simple: when you push out your baby, you engage the same muscles you use to have a bowel movement. In addition to this, your baby creates a lot of pressure on the rectum and colon as it squeezes through the birth canal. It's absolutely essential that

women do not become consumed by self-consciousness when this happens. Doctors are completely used to seeing this happen in the delivery room, as it happens to most women. What doctors do mind is that this self-consciousness can often prevent women from pushing properly, making everyone's job a lot more difficult. Just focus on delivering your baby and know there's no reason to worry about anything else.

5. **There's a possibility you'll throw up or be nauseous.** Not all moms experience this, but many do and it's completely normal. If you're using an epidural, which causes blood pressure to drop, this can bring on nausea or vomiting as it sets in. Though even if you aren't using an epidural, these side effects are still a possibility. While you're giving birth, many of your body's functions slow down or stop, including digestion. And if you have a lot of food in your stomach, it may need to come back up. If you'd like to minimize your risk of vomiting, stop eating and stick to water once you're in active labor. And in early labor, try to only eat light food.

6. **A lot of people will be there over the course of your labor and childbirth.** Although this depends heavily on the type of facility you'll be delivering at, for the most part, it takes more than two or three people to deliver a baby. If you're having your baby in a big hospital, expect to see many different faces over the course of labor and childbirth. Not only will you need a nurse or two, but you'll also need a midwife, the doctor, various assistants, and if your hospital is a teaching hospital, then possibly even medical residents. Don't be alarmed when you see more than a few new faces. It's all completely normal and everyone is just there to help.

7. **Your doctor may need to open you up wider.** To help get your baby out, your doctor may think it is necessary to give

you an episiotomy. This is when an incision is made along your perineum (the skin between your vagina and anus) so your baby can be delivered easier. Doctors usually do this for a good reason but in many cases, it is possible to opt out of it. Speak to your doctor about this beforehand, if you'd like to avoid an episiotomy. But also know that you may want one – it can move things along when you're running out of steam!

8. **You'll deliver far more than just a baby.** Don't worry, this isn't as scary as this sounds. After giving birth, mom is going to need to expel a few things that she no longer needs in her body, namely the placenta (also known as the afterbirth) and lots of blood and tissue. New moms are always alarmed by how much blood comes out of their body after birth; expect it and don't be nervous.

9. **Overwhelming happiness may not be your first emotion after giving birth.** After a physically and emotionally exhausting birth, and labor which may have lasted hours or days, it's normal for mom to be emotionally shut down. This is a normal response while extremely exhausted and it's important that everyone lets mom rest. And mom, too, should not be ashamed that she isn't jumping for joy after such a physically draining experience. Just give mom some time to recharge and she'll wake up with the incredible joy that everyone else is feeling as well.

10. **Childbirth is difficult on partners too.** Of course, it won't be nearly as much of a challenge as it is for mom – but that doesn't mean it isn't a challenge for dad or other birth partners! It isn't uncommon for nurses to take someone out of the delivery room because it's too upsetting to watch their loved one in so much pain. If this happens, do not fault your partner for having this reaction. Many partners do.

4 Things to Do for a Safer C-Section

There's no need to worry about your C-section. It's true that it comes with more risks than a vaginal birth, but this is true of all surgeries. Complications from cesareans are rare and women generally have a lot of control when it comes to avoiding these complications. Many new mothers are interested in the precautions they can take before and after their C-section. Here's what you can do to ensure you steer clear of the risks of a C-section.

1. **Wash yourself with antibacterial soap before surgery.** Doing this ensures that there is less bacteria in the area where you will be cut, therefore reducing your risk for infection – one of the biggest risks associated with C-sections.
2. **Do not shave your pubic hair yourself before surgery.** If it needs to be removed, it will be trimmed carefully by surgical staff. Shaving can increase your risk of infection.
3. **Keep warm the best you can.** Getting cold before or during a C-section can raise your risk of infection very slightly. Make sure you're snug and warm in all the blankets you need.
4. **Walk as soon as you can after surgery.** Yes, you will be sore, but walking shortly after surgery gets your blood moving again – and this is essential for reducing the risk of blood clots. Whatever you do, don't overdo physical activity. Just make sure you get some time on your feet to start the healing process.

The Lowdown on Epidural Anesthesia

When it comes to pain relief during childbirth, epidural anesthesia is the most prominently used. Not only is it administered for c-sections and vaginal deliveries, but it also relieves pain for a number of other surgeries and body pain from a prolapsed disc.

How is an Epidural Administered?

The epidural is injected with a needle into the lower back, specifically in the area around the spinal nerves. A local anesthesia is given in this same area prior to the epidural, so mothers do not feel too much pain from the second round of anesthetic. Epidurals numb the body below the place of injection, so mom's birthing pains are lessened significantly and yet she can still stay awake during childbirth or c-section. It takes roughly 15-20 minutes for the anesthetic to take effect. Since the bottom half of the body is numb, a catheter is usually inserted until the effects of the epidural wear off.

Why Should You Get an Epidural?

An epidural is completely optional for vaginal births. Many women claim they absolutely need it and others cope just fine without one. The biggest and most obvious advantage to the epidural is, of course, having a far more painless or, in some cases, *completely* painless delivery. Many women find the pain of childbirth unbearable and if labor was difficult as well, some mothers just can't handle anymore. Free of pain, many mothers find that they are completely clear-headed during labor.

Why Shouldn't You Get an Epidural?

There are a few reasons why some moms opt out of the epidural. Some women do not like the sound of the side effects, which can include headaches, nausea, urination during delivery and inability to control it for a short while afterwards, temporary nerve damage, and difficulty walking. Due to the lack of sensation in the lower half of the body, women under epidural anesthesia tend to also have a hard time pushing effectively during delivery. So even though birth becomes painless, an epidural can prolong the overall time of labor. After birth, the anesthetic still needs time to wear off, so mom won't be able to feel her legs for a short time after.

Like with most things, epidurals come with their own risks. There is always a small possibility (roughly 0.5%) that moms will develop a post-dural puncture headache – a severe headache that sets in anywhere from a day to a week after an epidural. The pain from this headache will become intense when upright in a seated or standing position but lessen when lying down. Accompanying the pain, there may also be nausea, vomiting, neck pain and an extreme sensitivity to light. Despite being painful, this is easily treated by a doctor.

Will an Epidural Affect the Baby?

Unfortunately, a lot more studies need to be done on this subject. There is some evidence to show that epidurals have a subtle effect on newborns, but this hasn't been explored in detail. What we do know is that epidurals do not harm a baby, as far as we know, and if there are any side effects, they are not serious. For example, some studies have shown that epidurals may lead to issues breastfeeding, namely with getting the baby to "latch on" to the breast – but this does no lasting damage to the baby.

7 Helpful Tricks for Pushing that Baby Out

1. **Push as if you're going to the bathroom, i.e. having a bowel movement.** This always throws first-time moms off! Naturally, they think that if they're trying to push a baby out and *not* go to the bathroom, they shouldn't be using those muscles. This is wrong! And this is why it's difficult to avoid having a bowel movement while giving birth. If it feels as if you're pooping, you're on the right track! Don't be embarrassed and just get it done.
2. **Use big focused pushes instead of smaller frantic ones.** Many first-time pushers try to conserve their energy and opt for light but frequent pushes. These will prove very ineffective

and may just prolong the time spent in labor. Put focus and a lot of energy into every push! Frequent and intense pushes are far better than prolonged pushes.

3. **Don't strain or push with your upper body.** This won't impact your baby's birth but it may leave mom with facial bruising or bloodshot eyes. When mothers let out an intense push, they instinctively pull their upper body into it as well. To avoid bruising in the upper body, push only with your lower body and do not strain your face too hard.
4. **Don't be afraid to try a different position.** Most women give birth lying on their back but other positions have proven much more helpful for getting a baby out. If lying on your back isn't doing the trick, try squatting upright. This way, gravity can assist with birthing your baby.
5. **Keep breathing and do not hold your breath for longer than a few seconds.** When in intense pain, many people naturally start to hold their breath. Resist doing this when you're giving birth. Take deep breaths whenever you can and especially before each big push.
6. **Don't push until you feel like pushing.** Being in labor doesn't mean you're ready to push. You'll know when you are! And when the time comes...
7. **Push when you feel like pushing!** Your body knows when the right time is. In fact, pushing is more like an involuntary response and reflex. You'll have to try hard to not do it. If you know you're fully dilated and the urge comes, go for it.

The Best Positions for Pushing with an Epidural

Epidurals will make the pain of childbirth a lot more manageable. In some cases, it may eliminate the pain entirely. Unfortunately, along with the elimination of pain, an epidural can also numb or diminish urges to push. These urges are very helpful when it comes to getting a baby out as they basically tell mom when she should be pushing. When mom can't tell what's happening with her body, pushing the baby out becomes a lot more complicated. Thankfully, there are many birthing positions that may make it easier on mom and baby. If you're taking an epidural, keep these positions in mind:

- Lying on the side.
- Kneeling by or at the foot of the bed while leaning over.
- Squatting with support from others.
- Lying on the back with legs in stirrups or supports.
- Upright sitting position.
- Half-sitting with knees pulled towards you.

7 Little-Known Things about C-Sections

1. **You'll still feel your baby coming out.** It won't be painful in any way but you'll still be able to feel a vague tugging at your abdomen. If you've had other types of surgery before, it is not too different from that.
2. **The surgical team may seem unusually casual.** Even though this is your first birth, the surgical staff taking care of you have done this plenty of times before. Many first time moms are taken aback by the casual and laid-back chatter amongst the staff. Learn to see this as a positive thing! It means everything is going exactly as planned so you can just relax.
3. **If you want to watch your baby come out, you can.** Even if you haven't included this preference in your birth plan, you can still ask to have this arrangement on the day. Just make sure you're ready to see a lot of blood!
4. **Your partner may not be prepared to see you cut open.** It's customary for doctors to warn birth partners about what they might see – and most will advise just focusing on your face –

but squeamish or not, partners sometimes can't resist the temptation to look. It's not the easiest sight to behold so be prepared to see your partner get a little pale!
5. **Doctors might strap you down.** This doesn't always happen but it isn't uncommon. Many mothers find this unusual but it's all to ensure the utmost safety. The last thing anyone wants is movement that makes surgery more difficult. The good news is you'll barely feel your arms and they may even unstrap you once your baby is out.
6. **The birth will be quick but the stitching up will take some time.** In fact, your baby will be out within the first ten minutes of the surgery starting. Stitching you up, however, can take up to 45 minutes. This said, many moms barely notice the time going by when they're getting sewn up. Why? Because they're just thrilled the baby is out!
7. **You'll be numb for quite some time.** Thanks to the pain medication, you won't feel it at all the first time you touch your C-section scar. It's also possible you won't feel a thing the first time your baby breastfeeds. This upsets some moms but there's no reason to be – trust me, you'll feel your baby breastfeeding *a lot* after this point. The most important thing is that you and your baby are healthy, and a long, beautiful journey lays ahead of you.

Chapter 7 - Postpartum Care

First-time mom, you are a pillar of strength. You've finally brought your baby into the world and now, no one underestimates the fortitude you clearly possess. The journey only continues. After the difficulties of pregnancy and childbirth, it's absolutely crucial that you get in the habit of taking care of yourself, as well as your baby. Being the strong mother you are, it'll come naturally to you to just power through no matter how you're feeling. While this is an admirable ability, this attitude shouldn't dictate your lifestyle from now on. Not only are you transitioning into a new big role, but your body is also healing.

To ensure you take care of yourself in the best way possible, here are some of the many things you can do to nourish your inner and outer well-being. Get used to listening to your body so you can better identify what you need at any given moment.

What Every Mother Needs to Do after Giving Birth

1. Get A Lot of Rest

Needless to say, mom is going to need to rest and recharge. This can be difficult when you have a newborn. You'll find that your baby wakes up every few hours, needing to be fed, so getting a solid 7-8 hours will be pretty much impossible. A good rule of thumb is to sleep whenever your baby sleeps. Even if sleep only lasts for an hour or two at a time, these hours add up and can really help.

2. Get Help from Loved Ones

Whether it's your partner, family, friends or all of the above, make sure you get all the help you need with household chores and other responsibilities. Ideally, everything in the home should be taken care of, leaving you to focus on feeding the baby and taking care of yourself, until you've had more time to recover.

3. Get Good Nutrition

So many nursing others end up neglecting their diet and nutrition because they are just so tired. This is where your loved ones come in. Get a family member or your partner to help you adhere to a healthy diet; this will aid you greatly on the road to recovery. According to lactation experts, it's best if mom eats whenever she is hungry – but ideally, she should be eating an overall balanced diet with the right amount of calories and fat. These include:

- Whole grains, such as whole wheat or oatmeal.
- Unpasteurized dairy products, such as milk or yogurt. If possible, stick to low-fat or fat-free options.
- Fruits in any form, including 100% fruit juice. Tired moms may find that juice or a smoothie is the best and easiest way to get their fill of fruit.
- Vegetables – ideally a variety of them, including leafy greens, legumes, orange, red, and starchy vegetables.
- Protein with less of an emphasis on meats, especially red meats. The best proteins for recovering new moms are beans, seeds, nuts, and fish. For other types of meat, make sure you're only consuming lean meat.

9 Completely Normal Long-Term & Short-Term Effects of Pregnancy and Childbirth

1. Hair Loss

Remember when pregnancy hormones gave you thick, lush hair? A drop in those hormones means you're going to experience the opposite. After giving birth, many moms go through a period of hair loss. But don't worry, this isn't forever. This shouldn't last for more than five months.

2. Hemorrhoids

There's going to be general soreness in your nether regions after birth; if you notice some of this pain coming from your anus, then there's a good chance that you have hemorrhoids. This swelling can make bowel movements even more difficult than they already are with an episiotomy wound or tearing. If your doctor hasn't already given you a stool softener, it's time to ask for one. If you'd like other forms of treatment, try an over-the-counter cream for hemorrhoids or wear pads that contain a numbing solution. Hemorrhoids are easily treated, so there's no need to fret about this one.

3. Incontinence

I warned you about this, didn't I? Pregnancy and childbirth can really pull a number on your pelvic floor muscles. When the muscles that control urination, bowel movements, and passing gas are stretched or injured, it can lead to some frustrating side effects. Most moms experience some level of stress incontinence, which is when a little urine leaks out while laughing, coughing, or sneezing. Incontinence tends to improve after a few weeks but it isn't uncommon to have some lasting effects. Hopefully, you've been practicing your pelvic floor exercises! If you haven't, try doing them now.

4. Contractions

While the worst contractions are long behind you, it's normal to experience some cramping after giving birth. These are called afterbirth pains and they'll be the most intense on the few days right after childbirth. These contractions are a natural result of your uterus returning to its regular prepregnancy size. After a few days, you can expect afterbirth pains to gradually fade away.

5. Constipation

In the days that follow childbirth, it is extremely common to have some constipation. This tends to be caused by anesthesia and pain-relieving medication given to you at the hospital. These can slow down the function of your bowels for a short period of time. Some mothers also find themselves constipated out of the fear and anxiety of hurting their perineum. Stay fully hydrated and eat fiber-rich foods to ease constipation. If you think it might be anxiety causing this problem, talk to your doctor about using a stool softener. Constipation generally isn't a real problem unless you've gone four days after birth without having a bowel movement. At that point, contact your doctor anyway.

6. Wider Hips

Many women discover their body shape has changed after giving birth. Namely, their hips seem slightly wider. While some of this is down to pregnancy weight gain that will subside after a few months, it isn't uncommon for a woman's shape to see some permanent changes. During pregnancy, a woman's pelvis bone structure changes to allow a baby to move smoothly through the birth canal. Not every woman will find that this change lingers on, but a significant number do.

7. Mood Changes

I'll say this now and remind you later: don't feel guilty about your mood swings! Many moms are under the mistaken impression that they'll pop out a baby and have impermeable joy. This is a total myth and it leads to a lot of needless shame for a mom that just needs a break. Yes, you'll feel happy but you'll also go through a rollercoaster of other emotions. It's a combination of hormones and the fact you're just exhausted after the last nine months. Don't be hard on yourself! We'll get more in-depth with this later on.

8. Lower Sex Drive

For the same reason the mood swings come, a lower sex drive is very common in postpregnancy. This is especially true for breastfeeding women whose estrogen levels plummet even more from feeding their baby. Most women claim it takes, on average, a year for their sex drive to return to its normal state. But some only feel these effects for a few months. These effects will vary from woman to woman, as with most changes.

9. Melasma

If you've noticed darkened patches of skin on your cheeks, forehead, and/or upper lip, then you have melasma – and you're not alone. Melasma is triggered by any change in hormones. 50-70% of pregnant women are affected by it and many find it lingers long after they give birth. Most signs of melasma fade after a year but you may find that some dark spots need further treatment. Before you seek out the high-strength skincare that is usually prescribed for melasma, wait until you're no longer breastfeeding your baby.

10. Darker Skin on the Areolas & Labia

As I mentioned in a previous chapter, a woman's areolas get darker and sometimes bigger during pregnancy. Some women find that their nipples and areolas remain this darker shade even after giving birth. This isn't the only thing that changes, however; the labia, too, can become a darker shade and you may even see this same darkening with moles.

How to Help the Body Heal from Birth

Every mother is sore and in pain after childbirth. Depending on the type of birth you had, you're likely aching in more places than one. C-section or vaginal birth, doctors recommend that you abstain from sex for a few to several weeks. Absolutely do not try to do it anyway or your body will pay the price.

Follow your doctor's instructions and there will be nothing to worry about. You're most definitely on the road to recovery already, but here are a few other things that you can do to speed up the healing process.

Caring for Your C-Section Scar

Your doctor or nurse should have given you some helpful instructions about how to care for your C-section scar. It all comes down to two things: clean and dry. Ideally, you should be cleaning it gently every day with a little bit of mild soap and water. After washing, pat the scar dry with a clean towel. Most doctors will tell you it is completely fine to apply some petroleum jelly or an antibiotic ointment to your scar. However, some doctors feel it's best to let it be after washing and drying, with no oil or ointment whatsoever. None of these practices will do harm to your scar so feel free to choose what feels right for you, or ask your doctor what his or her preferred approach is.

Whenever you can, let your scar air out; air can help skin injuries heal faster. In addition to this, try to wear loose clothing to avoid rubbing against your scar. Your doctor should have also mentioned this, but avoid all exercise, especially during the first several weeks.

If your scar shows signs of swelling or redness in the skin surrounding it, or starts oozing out any liquid, make sure to contact your doctor as soon as possible.

Caring for Your Perineum

Pregnancy Guide

The perineum tends to be one of the most sore areas after giving birth. Whether you had it cut during delivery or it tore naturally, you're likely eager for some relief. Using an ice pack on the area every few hours can work wonders – especially the day after giving birth. After urinating, take extra care to gently clean the area, as urine can irritate the cut or torn skin. Spray or lightly splash some warm water on the perineum to prevent irritation. Do this before and after urinating.

Improving Urinary or Fecal Incontinence

Hopefully, you've been doing the pelvic floor exercises in Chapter Three! These will have given you some strength against incontinence. If you weren't quite so diligent about it, that's okay! You can start doing them as soon as you feel you are well enough. These would take effect immediately, but if you stick with it, you'll see improvements soon enough.

Easing Painful or Sore Breasts

Aside from using lanolin ointment on your nipples, make sure to also let your breasts breathe after each feeding session. Being exposed to cool air can have a soothing effect on the skin. Some mothers find that using a warm compress or heating pad on sore breasts can really help a lot.

Soothing General Achiness 'Down There'

If the pain gets too uncomfortable, the use of painkillers is always an option, especially acetaminophen can help greatly with pain in the perineum. Other soothing methods include taking a sitz bath and using a heating pad. Many mothers also swear by witch hazel pads, which can be used in conjunction with an ice pack to ease pain in the vagina and/or postpartum hemorrhoids.

Everything You Need to Know About Postpartum Depression

The birth of a baby brings incredible joy into the lives of two lucky parents. It is entirely common, however, to feel a range of other emotions. With joy, there may also be fear and anxiety about being a good enough carer or parent. And mothers may even feel the 'baby blues' starting as soon as a couple of days after delivery. These feelings are very normal and for many mothers, the blues can disappear in just a couple of weeks. When the baby blues last for an extended period of time, however, this is called postpartum depression. The symptoms of postpartum depression include:

- A pervasive feeling that you can't bond with your baby.
- Complete depletion of energy.
- Insomnia or oversleeping.
- Loss of appetite or overeating.
- Withdrawal from close friends and family.
- Excessive crying spells.
- Strong feelings of being an inadequate or bad mother.
- Restlessness and anxiety.
- Mood swings or general depression.
- Guilt, shame, and feelings of worthlessness.

If these symptoms persist for over two weeks, it is essential that new mothers seek out help for postpartum depression. This is especially important if symptoms cross the line into postpartum psychosis, marked most notably by feelings of confusion, delusions or hallucinations, obsessive thoughts that revolve around the baby, paranoia, and perhaps even thoughts or attempts to hurt oneself or the baby. The longer these conditions are left untreated, the longer they will continue. Help from a medical professional can allow new mothers to get back to a healthy frame of mind so they can enjoy their new role, as they deserve.

9 Soul-Soothing Self-Care Ideas for a First-Time Mom

1. Invite a Friend Over

If you're feeling up to it, why not invite a friend over? Once your newborn is a little more settled in and you've had time to recharge, getting some time with a friend whose company you love can be incredibly healing. While your baby is napping, you could have lunch together in your home and enjoy a movie or TV show. This is also a great time to make new friends with other first time moms. If you know anyone else who just had a baby, this may be the perfect time to form a bond.

2. Enjoy a Warm or Hot Bath

This self-care method isn't just soul-soothing, but it's also body-soothing, especially for sensitive areas that are sore. Feel free to also dim the lights, play music in the background, or light candles if you'd find it more comforting. You can do this at all hours of the day, whenever you need it the most. Do it between your baby's naps or simply ask your partner to take over for a while. Since you're probably tired, just make sure you don't fall asleep in the tub!

3. Pamper Yourself with a Massage or Manicure

You deserve to pamper yourself, new mom! Many new mothers feel guilty when they take time away from their baby to get pampered – but this guilt needs to stop. As long as you're not doing this excessively, you're giving yourself exactly what you need to be the best mom for your baby. Your body has gone through *a lot*; let yourself sit back so you can be taken care of for a moment. Whether it's a massage, a manicure, or a pedicure, do something that allows you to be still and be soothed.

4. Write in a Journal

Many new mothers love taking up journal-writing after they've had a baby. Even those who have never had a journal before. Documenting these early days can be very special and some moms even do it with the intention of sharing the journal with their child once they are old enough. Writing can center the soul and allow us to sit, breathe, and observe our everyday lives. If it feels like everything is changing and you haven't had time to yourself, the act of writing and recording can feel very anchoring. Deciding to not share this journal with anyone is fine too. Allow yourself to just feel what you're feeling and give yourself a safe space in a private journal. Find a time each day or every other day to write an entry in your journal, perhaps during one of your newborn's morning naps.

5. Reconnect with your Partner

With a new baby in the mix, many couples become overwhelmed and forget to take time to themselves. I don't just mean sitting down to watch TV in silence, but to actually talk and discuss how they're doing with the new changes in their lives. Remember what you did before the baby came along. Talk about what you used to talk about, make light of funny scenarios, and laugh together. Foster and nurture your connection, and you'll both find yourselves soul-soothed.

6. Dive Back Into an Old Hobby or Interest – or Find New Ones!

You may have a new baby but that doesn't mean you have to discard your hobbies and interests. In fact, it may be emotionally and mentally beneficial for you to get back into them. Studies have shown that when we regularly do something that takes us away from our usual train of thought, it triggers anti-oxidation in our body and combats stress. If you enjoy knitting, get back into it during the times you have to yourself. If you'd like to start sketching or blogging, now's not too late to start. Take your mind away, momentarily, and let your body destress.

7. Treat Yourself to Fun Soap, Lotion & Other Body Care

Now's the time to indulge in body care goodness. Whether it's LUSH, Bath & Body Works, or something else, treat yourself to products that make your body and skin feel amazing. The time you get to yourself in the shower counts as self-care; get all the fun flavors or flavors you can find and let yourself be soothed. If you have a C-section scar or any kind of stitching or tearing on your perineum, make sure to not rub any of these products directly on these areas.

8. Go on Frequent Walks

Walking is a great way for a new mother to get some exercise. It's safe for her recovering body, allows her to get some fresh air, and it can also improve her mood. Practice this healthy habit any way that works for you. You could take your baby out in his or her stroller, or you could ask your partner to watch your little one while you get some time alone to destress with a leisurely stroll. It may seem like too simple an act to make a difference, but you'll be surprised by how clear-headed and relaxed you can be from a walk. The best part is it doesn't have to take long and you can do it almost anywhere. Bring some music and headphones for an even more relaxing walk.

9. Take Care of the Basics

Sometimes the best self-care just requires doing the basics and doing them well. Many overwhelmed new moms are so exhausted they forget to do this. Eat nourishing food that you love, drink lots of water, use a lovely scented soap in the shower, and get some rest during your baby's naps. If you're not up for socializing, free yourself from those responsibilities. Just focus on taking care of yourself in the most basic but essential ways.

Chapter 8 - Your Newborn Baby

Holding your first baby in your arms is an unparalleled experience. To think you created this new life with your own body! What utter magic. You're going to have a marvelous time getting to know this tiny little human, but as you'll quickly realize, it's not all tickles and cuddles. Tiny humans need a lot of care and comfort. Since they don't have mom's strength yet, they're still very delicate and vulnerable. This chapter is packed with information on how to properly care for a newborn baby. As your baby gets older, your techniques and strategies will evolve as well – but for now, keep a close eye on these crucial details.

11 Things You Should Know About Newborn Babies

1. **It's normal for their skin to be dry.** After all, they were submerged in a wet womb before promptly hitting the air. The dryness can sometimes be alarming to new moms and dads, but it's actually completely harmless and there's nothing you need to do about it.
2. **If your newborn is fussy, try to mimic the conditions of the womb.** Consider how it felt for the baby to be snug inside your body and try to recreate that same environment. Try swaddling or gentle swinging, and accompany this by a light whooshing or shushing noise. You may even find that a warm bath has a soothing effect on your newborn.
3. **Make sponge baths the norm for the first couple of weeks** – or specifically, until the umbilical cord falls off. A sponge bath makes it easier to keep the umbilical cord dry, which is what it needs to fall off quickly.

4. **Expect some bleeding when the umbilical cord falls off.** Just think of it as a scab peeling off. Blood is normal and it's no reason to be alarmed.
5. **Newborns are near-sighted.** Just after birth, a newborn baby can only see about 8 to 12 inches in front of their faces. Everything beyond that is blurry and cannot be distinguished. As the months pass, your baby's sight will gradually get stronger. At three months old, shapes and colors will be much clearer.
6. **Don't fret if your baby loses a bit of weight.** A few days after giving birth, it isn't uncommon for babies to lose about five to ten percent of their body weight. This is not a sign that your baby is underfed. In fact, you'll discover your baby has gained more weight after a couple of weeks past birth.
7. **Breastfed babies have less smelly poop.** A strange fact but it's true! Just after birth, all babies have the same type of poop. But once you establish a feeding routine and decide on how you'll find your baby, the nature of their poop will quickly change. What does it depend on? Whether they're formula-fed or breastfed. Remarkably, the poop of breastfed babies does not stink at all.
8. **It's normal for newborns to have birthmarks.** These will appear pink or peach-colored on their face or neck. Some parents are even surprised to see these marks get more red when they're in distress. Roughly a third of babies will have these marks, so it's usually no cause for concern. But if you notice skin discoloration or strange bumps, it's always best to speak to a doctor. Otherwise, these harmless pink marks tend to disappear within six months.
9. **Newborns can leak milk.** In fact, you may even notice that some newborns appear to have tiny raised breasts. This and any

milk leakage is completely normal, and will not last beyond a few weeks. The reason behind this occurrence is that newborns absorb some of mom's estrogen hormones while they're in the womb. In baby daughters, it can also lead to vaginal discharge or mini periods.
10. **Most newborns like facing the right side when they sleep.** And many experts think this may be linked to why most people are right-handed. Only about 15% babies prefer to face the left side when they sleep.
11. **They can remember what you ate while you were pregnant with them.** And most fascinating of all, this may influence their own personal flavor preferences. Everything that mom eats after four months of pregnancy affects the way their amniotic fluid tastes and they'll know instantly when this same flavor comes up again in mom's breastmilk. If mom ate a lot of meals with heavy garlic flavoring, you can bet that baby will be drawn to garlic later on.

6 Must-Know Rules About Formula-Feeding

1. **Do not reuse formula your baby doesn't finish, even if you refrigerate it first.** It becomes a breeding ground for bacteria after a certain time and this is not helped by storing it. If, however, you've prepared formula that your baby never even touches the nipple of, then it's safe to store for 24 hours. Do not do this if your baby has had his or her mouth on the bottle's nipple at all.
2. Do not use prepared formula that's been left out for more than an hour. The bacteria that grows beyond this time can make your baby ill.
3. **Store formula in the back of your fridge, which is where it is coldest** – but do *not* freeze formula. Freezing formula

negatively affects its texture and consistency. While this isn't dangerous, you baby will be far less likely to drink it this way.

4. **Serve formula as soon as it's prepared and warmed.** As soon as it has time to sit, bacteria starts to accumulate. Give it to your baby before it has time to become a breeding ground.
5. **Be a total clean freak when it comes to your baby's formula.** This is one of the few times it's completely appropriate to go nuts over every detail. Make sure you wash your hands before handling your baby's formula and the counter on which it's being prepared. In addition to this, always clean and then properly dry the lid of your formula. Like I said, be a clean freak!
6. **Do not heat up formula in the microwave.** Doing this will heat the formula up unevenly, making extremely hot spots in the solution which are likely to burn your baby's mouth. The best way to heat up formula is with a bottle warmer. If you don't intend on purchasing one, leave bottled formula to stand in a bowl of hot water for just a few minutes. This should do the trick!

Foods to Limit or Avoid While Breastfeeding

You may not be pregnant anymore, but if you're breastfeeding, your baby will still affected by what you eat and drink. For this reason, you'll need to watch what enters your body. Not everything on this list needs to be completely eliminated from your diet; you'll just need to moderate the amount you eat or do so with precaution. Foods you need to limit will not harm your baby in any way, but they may bring about an undesired reaction or behavior, making it more difficult for mom and dad to establish a healthy dynamic. It is important to note that every baby is different and some 'foods to limit' may be more compatible with your newborn.

Pregnancy Guide

Foods to Limit or Moderate

- Spicy Food

Hot spices can have an affect on how your milk tastes and interacts with your baby's system. Most babies can handle it, but in large amounts or too much frequency, it may induce, colic, gas, or even diarrhea. Some babies are less tolerant towards spice so always pay close attention to see what your baby can handle.

- Certain Herbs

Herbs such as peppermint, sage, thyme, oregano, and parsley should be used sparingly. While they aren't dangerous to the baby in any way, they are well-known to reduce a mother's milk supply. On the other hand, feel free to enjoy them if you're struggling with an oversupply of milk or trying to wean your baby off breast milk.

- 'Gassy Vegetables'

No mom should flat out avoid gassy vegetables, but in the early days, you may need to watch your baby to see how he or she reacts. Gassy vegetables include onions, broccoli, cabbage, cauliflower, peppers, and garlic; some babies can handle these just fine, but others can get extremely uncomfortable and gassy.

- Caffeine

Breastfeeding mothers still have to avoid caffeine, but they can consume about 100g more than they used to. This said, some moms choose to opt out of caffeine since it can give their baby sleep problems and make them very fussy. Remember that caffeine isn't just in coffee, it's also in chocolate, energy drinks, and certain teas.

- Alcohol

Doctors still say the safest option is to avoid alcohol, but breastfeeding mothers no longer *have* to. There are very reliable ways to get a drink in without it affecting the baby. Breastfeeding mothers should limit themselves to a small glass of wine or a half-pint of beer a day and absolutely no more than that. As with everything in your diet, alcohol can pass through your breast milk to your baby. It hasn't proven to be harmful in very small amounts, so it's essential that mothers limit how much gets through. They can do so by:

I. Waiting at least three hours after drinking to breastfeed the baby.
II. Drinking while breastfeeding, as it takes about 25 minutes for alcohol to enter breast milk.
III. Feeding the baby from stored breast milk when alcohol is still in mom's system.

It's also important that mothers stick to their alcohol limit per day. The more alcohol is consumed in one sitting, the longer it stays in your system.

Foods to Avoid

This one is simple: avoid all other foods that were in the 'Quit List' in Chapter 1. This means no high-mercury fish or unpasteurized dairy. If you're a seafood lover, make sure tuna, swordfish, mackerel, and shark are off your plate. And if you're a cheese nut, always check if it's pasteurized first.

How to Prevent Sudden Infant Death Syndrome

Sudden Infant Death Syndrome, also known as SIDS or Crib Death, is easily every parent's worst nightmare. It is the name given to the spontaneous death of a sleeping baby under one year-old. What makes SIDS even more harrowing is the fact that experts still aren't sure why it happens and there are no warning signs to watch out for. Unfortunately, there is no sure way to prevent SIDS, but you can take measures to lower your baby's risk. The good news is that these preventative measures seem to work; the SIDS rate has dropped by over 60% since they were made official to the public. Here are the best tips available on how to safeguard against SIDS:

1. **Lay your baby to sleep on a firm and bare mattress.** Even though it may seem as if an adorable little human needs something soft, firm mattresses are actually the best choice for SIDS prevention. Soft and fluffy paddings or quilts actually raise the chance suffocation or smothering. All you need is a firm mattress and a fitted sheet or a simple bassinet. And yes, this does mean *no* soft toys or crim bumpers.
2. **Put your baby to sleep on his or her back.** During the first year, they should never at any point be put to sleep on their side or stomach. If anyone else is taking care of your baby, it's important that you let them know this important detail as well. Many sitters believe that a fussy baby can be calmed if they're left on their stomach; whether or not this is true, the raised risk of SIDS means it is not worth finding out. Don't assume that every child care provider knows this and always let them know.
3. **Breastfeed your baby for as long as possible.** Even if you plan on formula-feeding eventually, see how long you can keep breastfeeding part of your baby's routine. Ideally, you should do this for six months, if you can. Remarkably, experts have found that breastfed babies have up to 50% of a lower risk of getting SIDS. The reasons why aren't very clear but it may be due to the fact that breast milk protects babies from infections, some of which could be responsible for SIDS. All this said, a breastfeeding mother that drinks alcohol actually raises her child's risk.

4. **Do not let your newborn sleep in the same bed as mom, dad, or another child.** While it's completely fine to cuddle and feed your baby in bed, avoid falling asleep together as this, too, raises the risk of suffocation and smothering. Accidents have occurred where a sleeping parent rolls against or onto their baby, restricting their breathing. Avoid this risk by sleeping in separate beds and not breastfeeding your baby in a position where you may fall asleep.
5. **Keep baby's crib in mom's bedroom.** Studies have shown that a baby who sleeps in mom's bedroom (but not in her bed) has a lower risk of SIDS. For this reason, experts tend to advise that newborns don't sleep in their own room until they're older than six months.
6. **Absolutely do not smoke around your baby.** Secondhand smoke is another major risk factor for SIDS. If a smoker is going to be around your baby, make sure that they do not smoke anywhere near the baby. If it helps, let them know of the risks so that they understand what's at stake.
7. **Make sure your baby doesn't overheat.** As you'd expect, overheating increases a baby's risk of SIDS. When your baby goes to sleep, have him or her dressed in comfortable clothes made of a light material. And as long as the room temperature is comfortable for an adult, then it's perfect for your baby.
8. **Don't give honey to an infant.** In very young children, honey can lead to an illness called botulism. While more research needs to be done on this subject, there is evidence to suggest that botulism is linked to SIDS.

And a final note: there are many products out there that wild claims about being able to lower a baby's SIDS risk – keep in mind that these are *just* wild claims. There is no evidence that any of these products, including electronic respirators and cardiac monitors, are effective or even safe.

It's Bath Time!

Bath time can be an incredibly fun and adorable experience with a newborn; you'll be pleased to know that this ritual only gets cuter as they get older. But when things get wet and slippery, the chance of an accident happening gets even higher. This is why it's very important that parents are prepared and attentive during their child's bath time. Follow these tips to make sure bath time is safe, efficient, and comfortable for your baby.

- Establish a bathtime routine

Choose a time of day that works for baby's bath time and try to stick to that routine. It's the best way to start setting your baby's body clock. Many moms prefer an evening bathtime routine since the time spent in water is very relaxing and sometimes makes baby sleepy. Over time, they begin to make the connection between bathtime and sleeptime, understanding that these activities go hand and hand. But this said, it's completely up to you and what works for your lifestyle. Morning bath routines are just as wonderful! And remember that just because you've established a routine doesn't mean you have to follow it religiously; if baby is hungry and bathtime needs to be postponed, that's fine too!

- Have everything you need closeby

Think of all the supplies you'll need while washing your baby and for right after, and have them within arm's reach. The last thing you want to do is to gather up your wet newborn mid-bath to rush to a different room. Make it easy on yourself! Have all bath time products and drying essentials ready nearby.

- Water should be warm but not hot

Before putting baby in the bath, test the water temperature with your elbow, one of the body's more sensitive areas. The water needs to be comfortably warm – not hot and not cold – around 98-100 °F. In order to get just the right temperature, I advise running the cold water first and the hot water after. Do not put your baby in running water. Being exposed to too-hot water for just a second can be enough to scald baby's skin. If you can, also try to keep the room temperature relatively warm, as naked babies can lose body heat very quickly.

- Don't leave your baby sitting in water for too long

Ideally, bath time should be at least five minutes and no longer than ten. When babies are left in water for too long, their skin becomes at risk of drying out, especially since it's already pretty dry. In extreme cases, babies can even catch hypothermia, a condition caused by losing body heat faster than you can produce it. And needless to say, you should also not leave your baby sitting or lying in water unattended. You must always stay present during your baby's bath.

- Use a mild and baby-friendly soap

A baby's skin is sensitive; for bath times, only use gentle soaps that are, ideally, free of fragrances. The chemicals and oils that are in mom and dad's soap are likely to irritate their skin – even if the packaging looks inviting! To safeguard against skin irritation, I'd even advise using just a small amount of soap and only using it towards the end of bath time. When a baby sits in soapy water for too long, irritation can also develop that way.

- Wash baby girls from front to back

This isn't just a tip for bath time, it is also an important piece of advice for diaper-changing. Whether you're wiping or washing a baby girl, you should always go from front to back. This is to avoid anything harmful from getting into her most sensitive area. To be extra safe, you should also steer clear of using soap on her vagina, as oftentimes this can lead to skin irritation.

- Do not put newborns in a bath seat or ring

In fact, all babies under one year-old should not be in a bath seat. The reason is simple: these babies are just too small for a bath seat. Too-little babies can easily slide out of the seat since they aren't yet able to fully support themselves. And on top of this, bath seats can easily collapse, potentially leading to the submersion of a baby's face in water. It's also possible for babies to get stuck in or under these unwieldy contraptions. At this point in your child's life, the support of mom or dad's arms are more than enough to keep them safe and comfortable. Sometimes 'simple' really is better.

By now, I don't need to tell you that raising a newborn is hard work. There's a lot of information out there about how to do it right – at the end of the day, what matters most of all is what's safest for your baby.

Enjoy these precious moments with your newborn baby. If there's anything that has struck me about having a newborn baby, it's this: time goes by so fast! In fact, the newborn stage doesn't seem to last long at all. Before you know it, you have a toddler and then a smart-mouthed kid (or at least I do!), and you're left wondering, "Where did all that time go?"

So, as stressed-out and exhausted as you are, take the time to snap a mental picture of these early days. You'll cherish these memories forever.

Pregnancy Guide

Conclusion

Congratulations on making it to the end of *First Time Mom*! One of the best things you can do as a new parent is to stay informed; that's what you've done by finishing this book! You are leaps and strides closer to being the best parent you can be for your little one. Many new moms feel overwhelmed by how much information there is to read and remember. Just know that your immediate concerns should be eating well, staying away from harmful activities, and taking care of yourself. To lighten the load off your shoulders, I even recommend passing this book on to your birth partner or closest family member. This way you can both be aware of the best way to take care of you and the baby.

I've walked you through the details of each and every trimester. By now, you'll know all about your expected symptoms and you'll have picked up some tricks about how to manage them. You'll know what supplements to include in your diet, how to control your pregnancy weight, and how to take care of your skin to minimize the chance of stretch marks. In the early days, your body will be going through some big adjustments; by now, you'll know what these changes are. If you feel like you need someone else on board for some extra support, go ahead and begin the search for a doula! Especially for a first-time mom, a doula can make a world of difference to your first pregnancy experience.

Remember to start your pelvic floor exercises in the second trimester – that is, if you've decided to do them. It's completely optional, but they'll be highly valuable in preventing incontinence. Preeclampsia symptoms can show up as early as the second trimester, so if you notice any unusual symptoms, refer back to the preeclampsia section to see how many signs you check off. You're probably okay, but reach out to a doctor immediately if you're unsure. It's always best to be safe!

When the third trimester rolls around, it's about time to start preparing for your big day and your new life with your baby. Decide whether you'd like to breastfeed or formula-feed your baby. Make sure you have everything or at least most of the things on the 'Necessities' list. You won't want to go out shopping when your newborn arrives, so it's best to get that out of the way now! You can also prepare for your big day by creating a birth plan, but this isn't necessary. It's just a way for you to establish what you want for your big day and to ensure those wishes are met.

If you have a doula, she'll be able to tell you when you're in labor and when you need to go to the hospital. If you don't, then make sure you pay close attention to what the most common labor signals are. You should also know how to tell the difference between Braxton Hicks contractions and real labor contractions. You don't want to end up going to the hospital for nothing!

Eventually, your big day will come and your little one will be ready to be born. Whether you plan on a vaginal birth or a C-section, childbirth is rarely easy. Stay fully informed about what you can expect. If you're having a vaginal birth, read up on epidurals so you know whether you'd like one. Keep in mind that you may change your mind at the last minute, if the pain is intense. There's nothing wrong with this!

You'll feel a rollercoaster of emotions in the days following your child's birth. There will be overwhelming joy, but many mothers also develop the baby blues and postpartum depression. Don't feel guilty or ashamed if you have your low moments. This is normal. Seek out help if you feel you may have postpartum depression. It's easily treated in this day and age. Take care of your emotional health and also take care of your physical well-being. Do not stress your body out or perform rigorous exercise for a while. Focus on eating well, sleeping, and nursing your baby. Get all the help you need from your friends and family. And remember that self-care is extremely important for the recovering first-time mom!

Of course, the journey doesn't end once you give birth. This may seem like a lot already, but all of this counts as step one. Motherhood begins here. When you have your newborn baby in your arms, it'll feel like a new day has started and in many ways, it has. No mother will ever be 100% prepared because every baby is different, so when all else fails, focus on the core things: baby's food, sleep, and safety – and yours as well. You're not alone in this! Refer back to this book whenever you need to and don't be afraid to ask your partner for help.

Welcome to the beautiful and empowering journey of motherhood, first-time mom! You've done an incredible job. I wish you and your new family happiness, health, and a lifetime of fun adventures together.

Pregnancy Guide

30 Day Meal Plan

Week 1

	Breakfast	Lunch	Dinner
Day 1	Oatmeal with blueberries, sliced apple, and a pinch of cinnamon.	A peanut butter and banana sandwich made with whole-wheat bread.	Salmon with a side of baked broccoli and potatoes.
Day 2	Greek yogurt and berries of choice.	A cooked-turkey wrap with swiss cheese, avocado, spinach, and hummus.	Cooked shrimp (deveined and peeled) with broccoli, cauliflower, garlic, and tomatoes in olive oil.
Day 3	A smoothie made of bananas, raspberries, chia seeds, and low-fat vanilla yogurt.	A baked potato with butter and cheddar cheese.	Pasta in a light olive oil or butter sauce with spinach, mushrooms, and pine nuts, topped with parmesan cheese.
Day 4	An omelette with cheddar cheese and toasted	An arugula and fig salad topped with balsamic	Pork chops, green beans, and mashed sweet potatoes.

Pregnancy Guide

		whole-wheat bread, lightly buttered.	vinegar, walnuts, and parmesan.	
Day 5	Granola with low-fat yogurt and berries of choice.	A spinach and cheese quiche with any salad of choice.	Chicken tenders in a lemon sauce, topped with parmesan, with a side of brussel sprouts.
Day 6	A peanut butter, banana, milk, and spinach smoothie.	Avocado toast with a sprinkle of salt and pepper.	Roasted chicken with baked baby potatoes, asparagus, and carrots.
Day 7	Broccoli and cheddar cheese omelette.	Creamy butternut squash soup.	Garlic, shrimp, and mushroom quinoa cooked in vegetable broth.

Week 2

	Breakfast	Lunch	Dinner
Day 8	Scrambled eggs on whole-wheat toast with baked beans on the side.	A chicken salad with sliced avocado, spinach, parmesan,	Beef liver, onions, and mushrooms with

Pregnancy Guide

		olive oil, and balsamic vinegar.	a side of brown rice.
Day 9	Oatmeal with two sliced bananas.	An egg wrap with cheddar cheese, spinach, and salsa.	Chicken cutlets in a mushroom sauce with peas and carrots.
Day 10	A smoothie made of bananas, pears, chia seeds, and low-fat vanilla yogurt.	Broccoli and pea soup with optional whole-wheat toast for dipping.	Lamb chops with a side of asparagus and sweet potato wedges.
Day 11	Greek yogurt and berries of choice.	A baked potato with cottage cheese.	Broccoli, spinach, and sweetcorn pasta bake with cheese.
Day 12	Spinach and cottage cheese omelette.	A peanut butter and banana sandwich made with whole-wheat bread.	Chicken soup with carrots and celery.
Day 13	Low-fat yogurt with sliced mango and banana.	A cooked-turkey wrap with swiss cheese, avocado, spinach, and hummus.	Salmon with a side of kale cooked in lemon and garlic.

| Day 14 | Granola with low-fat yogurt and berries of choice. | Spinach and edamame salad with grated carrots, parmesan shavings, and sweet corn with a citrus dressing. | Mushroom and chicken risotto made with brown rice. |

Week 3

	Breakfast	Lunch	Dinner
Day 15	A smoothie made of kale, avocado, bananas, pineapple, and chia seeds.	A baked sweet potato stuffed with spinach, avocado, and topped with a sunny side up egg.	Pesto pasta with garlic, peas, and sun-dried tomatoes.
Day 16	Whole-wheat waffles topped with honey and sliced banana.	A walnut, pear, and feta cheese (pasteurized) salad.	Spaghetti bolognese.
Day 17	Sunny side up eggs with a side of mushrooms, spinach, and tomatoes.	Lentil soup with carrots, garlic, potatoes, carrots, and parmesan shavings on top.	Garlic, shrimp, and mushroom quinoa cooked in vegetable broth.

Pregnancy Guide

Day 18	Broccoli and cheddar cheese omelette.	Creamy butternut squash soup.	Chicken thighs baked with artichoke, peas, garlic, and onions.
Day 19	Whole-wheat toast with banana and peanut butter or other nut butter.	Feta, spinach, and mushroom quiche.	Pork chops, green beans, and mashed sweet potatoes.
Day 20	A peanut butter, banana, milk, and spinach smoothie.	A chicken salad with sliced avocado, spinach, parmesan, olive oil, and balsamic vinegar.	Grilled salmon in a buttery lemon sauce with a side of chopped baby potatoes and asparagus.
Day 21	Avocado toast with a sprinkle of salt and pepper.	An egg wrap with cheddar cheese, spinach, and salsa.	A mushroom, spinach, celery, and cheese pasta bake.

Week 4

	Breakfast	Lunch	Dinner

Pregnancy Guide

Day 22	Spinach and cottage cheese omelette.	An arugula and fig salad topped with balsamic vinegar, walnuts, and parmesan.	Meatballs in tomato sauce with a side of mashed potatoes and broccoli.
Day 23	Oatmeal with blueberries, sliced apple, and a pinch of cinnamon.	Broccoli and pea soup with optional whole-wheat toast for dipping.	Chicken tenders in a lemon sauce, topped with parmesan, with a side of brussel sprouts.
Day 24	Sunny side up eggs with a side of mushrooms, spinach, and tomatoes.	A peanut butter and banana sandwich made with whole-wheat bread.	Cooked shrimp (deveined and peeled) with broccoli, cauliflower, garlic, and tomatoes in olive oil.
Day 25	Granola with low-fat yogurt and berries of choice.	A baked sweet potato stuffed with spinach, avocado, and topped with a sunny side up egg.	Beef liver, onions, and mushrooms with a side of brown rice.
Day 26	Egg, bean, and cheese breakfast burrito.	Spinach and edamame salad with grated carrots,	Mushroom and chicken risotto

		parmesan shavings, and sweet corn with a citrus dressing.	made with brown rice.
Day 27	A smoothie made of kale, avocado, bananas, pineapple, and chia seeds.	Avocado toast with a sprinkle of salt and pepper.	Chicken cutlets in a mushroom sauce with peas and carrots.
Day 28	Sliced peaches and mango in low-fat yogurt.	A pork and spinach salad with figs, red grapes, balsamic, honey, and pasteurized goat or feta cheese.	Pesto pasta with garlic, peas, and sun-dried tomatoes.

Week 5

	Breakfast	Lunch	Dinner
Day 29	Oatmeal with two sliced bananas.	Sandwich made of whole-wheat bread with artichoke, spinach, swiss cheese, sliced red peppers and sun-dried tomatoes.	Roasted chicken with baked baby potatoes, asparagus, and carrots.

Pregnancy Guide

| Day 30 | A peanut butter, banana, milk, and spinach smoothie. | Lentil soup with carrots, garlic, potatoes, carrots, and parmesan shavings on top. | Chicken thighs baked with artichoke, peas, garlic, and onions. |

Snack List

Any Week

A bowl of mixed fruit	Chips and guacamole	Roasted tomatoes topped with parmesan	Banana bread
Cheese (pasteurized) and Crackers	Almonds	Kale chips	Dried fruit and nuts
One or two hard-boiled eggs	Cottage cheese	Cucumber and carrot sticks with peanut butter	Sweet potato chips
Edamame	Bananas	Low-fat yogurt and cereal fortified with iron or fiber	Hummus and pita bread
Homemade iced tea with lemon	Oatmeal and raisins	Orange slices	Black bean and cheese quesadilla

No-Cry Baby Solution

Table of Contents

Introduction **119**

Chapter 1 - The Basics of Baby Sleep **123**
    Baby Sleep Cycles By Age 123
    How Do Sleep Cycles Differ By Age? 126
    5 Fascinating Facts About Your Baby's Sleep 129
    Important Precautions To Keep Your Baby Safe As They Sleep 131
    What About Co-sleeping? 133
    What About You? How To Manage On Broken Sleep 134

Chapter 2 - Getting Organized **138**
    Everything You Need for Your Baby's Sleeping Area 138
    Where Should Your Baby Sleep? 141
    Sleep Associations: What They Are & How They Can Help 141
    What is a Sleep Log? 148

Chapter 3 - Baby Sleep Problems **149**
    8 Common Baby Sleep Problems by Age & How to Manage Them
    149
    Fixing Less Common Reasons for Poor Sleep 153
    What Your Baby's Sleep Habits Mean 156

Chapter 4 - Preparing for Sleep Training **159**
    Hard Truths about Sleep Training that All Parents Must Know . 160
    Is Your Baby Ready for Sleep Training? 164

How to Choose the Right Sleep Training Method for Your Baby 167

Chapter 5 - Sleep Training Success 169

4 Transformative Sleep Training Methods 169

Sleep Training in More Detail: Here's How 173

How to Make Sure Your Baby Sleeps Through the Night 175

Why Sleep Training Fails & What to Do 176

Chapter 6 - It's Naptime! 179

Strategies for a Successful Naptime 180

What if Your Baby Won't Nap? 183

Chapter 7 - No Problem Too Big 185

Understanding Sleep Regressions by Age 185

How to Deal With Sleep Regressions 188

6 Must-Know Sleep Strategies for Single Parents 190

Two Babies, Many Solutions 193

Chapter 8 - Completing Your No-Cry Toolkit 198

How to Soothe a Crying Baby 198

Baby Crying Patterns by Age 200

5 Effective Remedies for Colic 201

Helping a Sick Baby Get Restful Sleep 204

Conclusion 209

Introduction

Lack of sleep is one of the things many parents find most unbearable when they come home with a new baby. And for a certain amount of time, it's simply part and parcel of being a new parent. But there are things you can do to make your baby sleep better, and this book will give you all the information you need to enjoy more peaceful nights with your baby or toddler.

By the end of it, you should feel ready to make the right choices for your family about sleep training, along with setting up a daily routine, handling naps and illness, and dealing with a crying baby. I have tried here to distil both everything I have learned from raising two babies, and everything that the parenting experts know about babies, toddlers and sleep.

Sleep training isn't always easy, and it can lead to a few upset nights. A crying baby is hard for any parent, and if you've picked up this book because you have tried and failed to get your baby to sleep, you have my sympathy. Learning to fall asleep, and stay asleep is something that comes more naturally to some babies. But for others, unfortunately, it takes time and effort on the part of often exhausted parents to support their baby to sleep deeply and wake up refreshed and happy. Add in curveballs such as colic and common childhood illnesses, plus parents dealing with more than one baby, or single parenthood, and it's no wonder new parents are struggling. If this is you, you're no doubt exhausted and wondering what to do next – should you try sleep training, controlled crying, or some other technique you haven't read about yet? Are you doing something wrong? Is there something wrong with your baby? What is the secret of those mothers who have such 'good' babies; those who sleep through the night without complaint?

Rest assured, it is completely normal to ask all of these questions throughout your parenting journey. But please know that sleep problems are also totally normal with babies and toddlers, and over time things will improve. Babies simply need to adjust to the world they've arrived in, and some find this easier than others. This doesn't make them 'good' or 'bad' babies – it just makes each of them unique! Sleep problems in the early years are simply part of being a parent, and don't mean you are doing anything wrong. Sometimes, working around the poor sleep and finding ways to cope is your best option, and I will show you how to do that in the chapters to follow, along with safe and gentle sleep training options.

If you are due to have your first baby soon and want to get ahead with your parenting skills, this book will also be very useful and make those early days a little easier.

The best training is on-the-job, and as a mother who has raised two babies, I have been through the early, sleep-deprived days of living with a new baby, and know what worked for me. It may not be exactly what works for your baby – that is for you to discover. What is easy for one baby may not be easy at all for another, which is why it can be frustrating to receive so many different pieces of advice from well-meaning outsiders who don't know your baby as well as you do. Your instincts about what your baby needs are always worth listening to. Let them guide you as you find your way, and remember, even if people sound like they know so much more than you, everyone who parents is mostly winging it.

I don't try to offer my readers a perfect one-size-fits-all solution (which, when it comes to parenting, doesn't exist anyway). What I offer to you instead is a range of strategies to try, all based on sound research and the latest findings around baby sleep. All are based on both looking after my own babies and doing my own extensive research and reading around baby sleep. As someone who looks back on those sleep-deprived early days with mixed feelings, I always think of things I could have done better. Personally, with my first baby, I let the broken nights go on for far too long. With my second, I was more confident about taking charge, and he was a better sleeper from an earlier age.

Read on to discover all of the different things you can try to get your baby to sleep better. When you try these approaches, you can look forward to a less fretful and exhausted baby who will be far more engaged and happy in his or her waking hours. The other, very important, benefit will be for you – with more sleep and less time trying to get your baby to sleep, you'll feel so much better, have more energy and be able to get on with the business of living alongside your baby.

As with anything to do with your baby, it's always worth getting an expert opinion if there's anything that's bothering you. Help is out there, and you only have to ask. But for many parents, it's simply a matter of knowing what to expect and how you can guide your baby in the right direction.

I will also cover in detail all of the things you need to think about in relation to safe sleep – the equipment you need, where your baby should sleep, and how to avoid any accidents. We'll cover strange sleeping habits, how to keep a sleep log and how to carry out sleep training, should you feel it's what you need for your own and your family's well being. Nap times, sleep regression, and getting your baby to sleep well when she is sick are other areas you may find helpful at particular times on your journey. And we'll look at sleep issues for single parents, as well as those looking after more than one baby.

What I offer are not clear solutions, but a framework and guidelines for you to try, to see what works for you. When it comes to babies and toddlers, this is the only sane approach! Rest assured that by establishing routines and a gentle timetable around sleep, as well as some consistency, you will be well on your way to better nights.

So settle back, and work through this book in your own time, taking note of what works for your baby, leaving behind what doesn't, and may trying things a little further on down the track – sometimes your baby just needs a little more time.

I promise that by the end of it, you'll have many new ideas to work with, and will be starting to see the light at the end of the tunnel. What I don't want you to do is fall into despair about your baby's sleep – these precious months when your baby is small will pass quickly, and ideally there should be many moments of joy for you, too.

Let me assure you again that there are many ways in which you can help your baby become a better, longer sleeper. Please know that when this happens, your daily life together will become so much easier. It's also worth remembering that not all problems can be solved by you, but by the passing of time – your baby will grow up a little, learn new skills, and suddenly what was bothering you about their sleep has simply stopped happening. This is one of the most amazing things about parenting – watching as your child grows up, develops, learns new skills and becomes their own person. Each stage brings its own rewards along with the questions.

As well as helping your baby adjust to the world, you also have to take charge constantly as a parent, always noting what works for your particular baby. Sleep is one of the key areas you will need to focus on and feel confident about as you start your new life with your baby. And as a parent, acting with consistency and confidence is often the key to success.

Here is a guide to help you do just that.

Chapter 1 - The Basics of Baby Sleep

In this section, we'll touch on baby sleep cycles by age, so you can understand your baby's sleeping habits better. Babies change so quickly at this stage of life as their brains and bodies grow rapidly. Having a basic understanding of what to expect from your baby's sleep at each stage, and what you'll need to wait a little longer for, can be both helpful and reassuring to new parents.

Like everything else they have to master, babies need to **learn** how to sleep at night and stay awake during the day – it isn't something they can do from day one. It's also helpful to know that the wakefulness and unsettled sleep of a tiny newborn is partly a survival mechanism to keep them from falling too deeply asleep when they need to feed regularly and their lungs are still so new. Better sleep does come with time, and this is something all parents need to accept to some extent. What you can do, though, is to understand what to expect at each stage, and in later chapters we'll look at how to nudge your baby in the direction of good sleep habits.

In this chapter we'll also give you five fascinating facts about your baby's sleep. And finally, we'll cover the all-important precautions you can take when setting up your baby's sleeping area to keep him or her safe during naps and night time sleeping.

Ready? Let's get started.

Baby Sleep Cycles By Age

As a rough guide to work with, here's how much sleep babies and toddlers will need over a 24-hour period, varying between naps and longer sleeps at night.

Newborns: 16 hours, though it can be as little as eight and as much as 18

Three-month-old babies: around 15 hours

Two years plus: around 12 hours

Of course, as with everything, these times can vary between individual babies, and you'll quickly gain a sense of your own baby's sleep patterns. You'll also soon learn to value their sleep and do whatever you can to protect it, as it results in a much happier, more contented baby in their waking hours. And not only will a well-rested baby be more enjoyable and easy to be around, regular, deep sleep is essential for their growth and development.

One of the biggest shocks I received when I brought my first baby home from the hospital was when I tried to put him to bed on that first, exhausted night. *That was all pretty intense*, I thought to myself, *but at least now we can all have a good night's sleep and see where we are in the morning.*

For some reason, I simply assumed that because we were home, life would return to normal. He would understand that it was late and we were going to sleep now, right?

Of course, it didn't work out that way. The minute I turned off the light, my baby was wide awake and screaming for two hours solid as I tried to feed him, soothe him, comfort him – and get him back to sleep. Many unsettled nights followed, and it took me a while to get that full night's sleep I was expecting, but eventually, sleep and sanity returned. Sorting out feeding problems helped a lot, but much of it was due to him being so new to the world and unsettled by everything and everyone around him.

What I also soon realised from talking to my midwives and my own research was that newborns have no sense of night or day. To some extent, their sleep patterns are governed by their mother when they are in the womb, and the rise and fall of her own activity and hormone levels. But once they are born, their mother's movements no longer dictate their sleeping and waking times, and they need to establish their own sleep habits in time with the outside world.

You may notice that your baby seems particularly alert at night, which is totally normal for newborns. This will generally start to get better at around six weeks old, which is when the intensity of the newborn phase – the screaming, colicky hours and the unsettled behaviour – will often start to ease a little generally. It can be helpful to think of the first three months as a 'fourth trimester' when your baby is still adjusting to life outside the womb, and keep your environment as peaceful as you can, particularly if you have an unsettled, nervous baby (if you do, you'll know what this means.)

Having said all that, you may also wonder if there are there any ways of speeding up this process of getting newborns into a normal day-night sleep cycle? Yes! There's lots you can do. Playing with your baby and taking him outside in the daytime, and creating a quiet, dim, even boring, environment at night, will help him to learn that night is for sleeping. As adults, our sleep is governed by circadian rhythms – we feel alert during the hours of daylight, especially if we go outside and expose ourselves to natural light soon after waking, and at night time, when the lights begin to dim, our bodies produce melatonin, which readies us for sleep.

Your baby will soon do the same, but in the meantime, it's best to simply allow for the broken sleep, let other people take care of you, don't try and do too much or worry about "getting into a routine." For now, as much as you can, simply enjoy the precious newborn bubble. You can and will sleep later, I promise!

How Do Sleep Cycles Differ By Age?

Adult sleep cycles consist of deep 'soundless' sleep and REM or active sleep, which is also the dreaming phase of sleep and essential for healthy brain function, as it's when your brain essentially puts all its files in order. During REM sleep, the body is temporarily paralysed, but brain activity is noticeable, with irregular breathing and eye movements. An adult sleep cycle will last about 90 minutes, and at the end of it we either wake up or start a new cycle. Baby's sleep cycles are slightly different, and it helps to be aware of this.

Newborns (birth to three months)

A newborn will cycle between quiet and active sleep, and each cycle is shorter than an adult sleep cycle at about an hour long, up until around nine months of age. Unlike adults, babies will **begin** with active sleep, which is similar to REM in adults, and are more likely to wake up in this stage, particularly if they jerk and startle themselves. Around half of their sleep is spent in 'active sleep', compared to only 20 per cent for adults. While babies are asleep, their movements during this sleep may mean that the adult assumes they are waking up. But often, if they are left alone at this point, they will continue to sleep. This need to be 'held together' to fall into a deep sleep is why many babies respond well to firm swaddling, up until the age of about two months.

Around halfway through the sleep cycle, the baby will settle into a quiet sleep, with slower breathing, stillness and no eyelid fluttering. This is the end of the sleep cycle, after which the baby will either awaken, or begin a new cycle of active sleep. You will soon start to recognise the quiet sleep, which is less unsettled. However, very small babies tend not to have periods of long, deep sleep as older babies do.

By three months of age, rather than starting in REM or active sleep, babies will start a sleep cycle in deep sleep, like adults, which can make it easier for them to fall and stay asleep.

You'll find that once your baby starts onto solid food, around six months, their sleep will improve even more, and once they start moving independently they will tire themselves out more and sleep even better.

Newborns will tend to sleep off and on throughout the day, and while you can't control this completely, you can work around it and gently guide them towards sleeping at night and being awake during the day, with a couple of naps in between.

Newborns are also often quite light sleepers and will spend about half their time in active, not deep sleep. Because they are so small, their bellies can't hold much food so they will wake regularly to feed – as they grow, they will wake less often and will eventually 'sleep through' until (early) morning.

You'll also notice that a "good sleeper" won't necessarily stay that way. Newborns may start off sleeping very deeply and regularly, but at around three weeks they will start to become less settled -- sleeping less and crying more, often for no apparent reason. Around this time you may see one longer sleep of up to five or six hours, a couple of three hour sleeps, several two hour sleeps and five or six hours of drowsing, crying, and catnapping. No wonder parents of newborns are exhausted from all that broken sleep!

Infants (three to 11 months)

By three months, your baby may have settled into a regular routine, with a morning and afternoon sleep and sometimes an extra one, too. The morning sleep tends to be quite long, with one or two afternoon naps to follow before bedtime.

You can expect your baby to sleep for around 14-15 hours a day, with some babies sleeping for up to eight hours at night.

The active sleep phase is reduced, and they will start to sleep more deeply. You can expect them to wake at least once at night, with some babies waking every three hours for a feed.

At around six months, the total amount of sleep a baby has per 24 hour cycle will reduce to about 13 hours a day in total. The naps will also reduce – many babies drop the morning nap first (a sad day, but it also means you can go out more easily in the mornings!), but continue to have one or two afternoon sleeps. However, many children will continue having an after-lunch nap well into toddlerhood.

At around six months of age, babies will also begin to move towards a more typical sleep cycle, with longer cycles and less time in active sleep. Gradually, over time, they will build up to sleeping for a solid eight to 12 hours of uninterrupted sleep.

Babies at this age will also usually sleep better at night, though some may wake up and need to be settled back to sleep, often with a feed. Separation anxiety, which appears at this age, can also cause some babies to feel more clingy and wake in the night for reassurance, particularly if they have been separated from you during the day.

Establishing daytime and bedtime routines and creating a flexible structure can help your baby to get to sleep at night. We will cover all of this in detail in the chapters that follow.

Toddlers (12 to 36 months)

Around 12 months, your baby will start to move into toddlerhood. With this increased maturity, and more movement and activity in their daily life, they will be sleeping better at night and only wake up once or perhaps twice at night.

By the time they are around two, they will need approximately 12 hours' sleep over a 24-hour period, although they may have longer sleeps during growth spurts and developmental leaps – if this happens, work around it, as they really do need as much sleep as they can get at this age, when their brains are growing so quickly. We will cover the sleep regression that sometimes comes with growth spurts in later chapters. Sometimes, I would notice my toddler having an especially long, deep sleep, and waking up with a new skill that I hadn't seen before – it was as if the extra sleep had actually been an intense training session for a developmental leap.

5 Fascinating Facts About Your Baby's Sleep

1. The more they sleep, the more they sleep

An overtired, fretful baby can find it difficult to get to sleep, then find it hard to enjoy being awake, creating a cycle of bad sleeping. But good sleep creates more of the same. So keeping a baby awake when they are tired, to try and make them sleep better at night, will actually have the opposite effect. It seems counterintuitive, but a wired, overtired baby will find it harder to get to sleep than one who is put to bed earlier. Prioritising your baby's daytime sleep and getting into a regular routine is the best way of working towards better nights, and this is what we will focus on throughout this book.

2. Morning light promotes good sleep

Taking in natural light in the daytime, and creating a dimly lit environment at night, will stimulate the production of melatonin, a hormone that promotes sleep. This works for adults as well as babies – going outside and getting some natural light on your face soon after you wake up can be helpful if you suffer from insomnia as it 'sets' your body clock. Be sure to get outside with your baby – for a walk around the park, to the shops, or just out in your back garden – every day, so that they start to set their body clocks as quickly as possible. As we'll cover in later chapters, the variety and stimulation babies get from being outside is also an essential and easy aid to encourage better sleeping at night.

3. Babies take longer to reach a deep sleep – around 20 minutes.

Because babies start off in active, not deep sleep, they can move and grimace a lot in their sleep. So even if your baby seems unsettled, leaving them in peace will often result in them reaching deep sleep eventually. If you can, try to resist rushing in to soothe or pick them up when they first fall down – they may seem upset, but in fact they are busy falling asleep, or very close to it. If you find this difficult, force yourself to go and have a five-minute shower. You won't be able to hear any crying, you'll get five minutes to yourself, and you may just come out and find that your baby has fallen asleep in your absence.

4. Night waking are essential to their survival.

While it can be frustrating being woken through the night, your baby needs to wake up to fill their tiny belly. Once they are a little bigger, their sleep cycles will lengthen and you won't have such broken nights. They also may wake up suddenly due to a startle reflex and getting them back to sleep can be difficult. As mentioned earlier, some parents find that swaddling their baby in a soft blanket or sheet can hold them still and help them settle and stay asleep for longer. Swaddling is easy and often helps with broken sleep – look online for videos of how to swaddle a baby.

5. Babies learn as they sleep.

During REM sleep, research shows that blood flow to the baby's brain increases, as their brains work hard to integrate all the new information they have been given that day. Sleep is essential to brain development, so the more you can learn about sleep techniques and help your baby to achieve them, the better. During REM sleep you may notice your baby twitch, breath irregularly and move their eyes. They stay in REM sleep for about half of each cycle, which may be because at this age, they have so much learning to do. For this reason, too, you should avoid waking a sleeping baby as much as possible (as if you would!).

Important Precautions To Keep Your Baby Safe As They Sleep

To keep your baby safe as they sleep, here are some essential guidelines to follow. We will cover some of the points in more detail in the following chapters.

- Always put babies to sleep on their backs, both at night and when they have daytime naps. Once they are a little older, they may find their own position as they move around throughout the night, but always put them to bed on their back.

- Sleeping should be done only on a firm surface, such as a mattress in a safety-approved crib or bassinet. Avoid soft fluffy blankets or cushions.

- It's recommended that you share a room with your baby for the first six months. A cot attached to your bed, with an open side that can be dropped down for feeds, is a solution that will ensure everyone gets enough sleep. Babies often sleep better if they know their parent is in the room, although once you attempt sleep training you will need to move your baby (or yourself) into another room, at least temporarily – more on this later.

- Use a fitted sheet and keep all soft objects, toys, padding and pillows away from the sleeping area. A zip-up sleeping bag with a fitted neck and armholes is a safe option for sleep as it can't cover the baby's face. These sleeping bags come in different thicknesses so you can choose the right one for your climate and time of year. They also serve as a useful sleep cue, telling your baby it's time to go to bed – again, more on sleep cues later.

- Never smoke around your baby, or allow other people to smoke in areas where your baby spends time. If someone has been smoking, they shouldn't hold a small baby. Smoking is associated with an increased risk of SIDS, so keep your environment completely smoke-free, and avoid it when you are out, too, especially if your baby was sick or premature at birth.

- Never fall asleep with your baby on a sofa or other area apart from the safe sleeping area. If you want to sleep close to your baby, set up an open cot next to you bed so the baby is close but safely out of the way. Planning co-sleeping like this is far safer than accidental co-sleeping, particularly when everyone is exhausted and can fall asleep very deeply.

- Never sleep near your baby if you have been drinking alcohol or are otherwise under the influence of drugs, or particularly exhausted. And never allow others who are under the influence of drugs or alcohol to fall asleep near your baby either. Pets should not share a sleeping area with babies, either.

- Keep an eye on the temperature of the room and ensure that it remains comfortable – not too hot or too cold. Keep your baby's head uncovered, and dress them in the same amount of clothing you would wear to bed. Overheated babies are at an increased risk of SIDS.

- Ensure everyone looking after the baby, or living in the house, is aware of safe sleeping practices, too. And finally, babies should never be left alone to sleep in cars, or in car seats, or unsupervised in prams.

What About Co-sleeping?

Some parents choose to co-sleep with their babies, and find that it works very well. Others don't choose to co-sleep but find instead that it chooses them, as their baby will not settle anywhere else but close to them at night. If you do choose to co-sleep, ensure that you are doing so safely. Sharing a bed is not safe if the baby is sharing a bed with a smoker, or if there are adult blankets that may cover the baby, or if the parent is drunk, drugged, obese or very tired.

If you do choose to co-sleep, ensure that your mattress is very firm, and that the baby cannot fall off the bed (a mattress on the floor is the safest option.) Put the baby on one side of the bed, not between two adults, dressed in a sleeping bag, not covered in adult blankets, and ensure that everyone knows the baby is in the bed.

You should also be aware that the risk of Sudden Infant Death while co-sleeping is most common in the first eleven weeks. Personally, at this age, I had my babies in a cot next to my bed, with one side removed, so there was no chance of me rolling onto them, but they were close by. Once they were older, they sometimes ended up next to me in bed, but for the most part they were in their own safe space. As with everything, it's always worth talking to your doctor and child health nurse before making a decision that works for you and your family. As mentioned earlier, accidental or unplanned co-sleeping, when you fall asleep with your baby unintentionally, is more dangerous than planned co-sleeping.

So now you know the basics of baby sleep from birth to toddlerhood, and know what you can expect in terms of sleep quality and length at each age. You also know how to set up a safe sleeping area for your baby. Let's move on to ways you can encourage deep, refreshing sleep for your baby so that he or she thrives and is happier in the daytime. But first, let's look at how to manage as a new parent on broken sleep.

What About You? How To Manage On Broken Sleep

Now that we've established that you won't be getting a full eight hours' sleep a night for some time, let's have a quick look at how you can help yourself through these early days. This time will pass, and you will sleep again, but it's important to go easy on yourself and not feel like you have to be your normal, well-rested self. Personally, I found the broken sleep and tiredness to be the hardest part of being a new parent. I couldn't hold proper conversations, I felt flat and exhausted a lot of the time, and I couldn't seem to think clearly or plan for the future. In retrospect, I wish I'd gone a bit easier on myself – napped more, gone to bed earlier, and not worried so much about the future and "getting everything under control." If you find you are really struggling, always seek help early from your doctor, in particular if you find you can't sleep yourself, even at night time.

Some baby experts refer to the first three months after the baby's birth as a Fourth Trimester. By this, they mean it's a time when you are still very much in the pregnancy and birth bubble, and should be resting and nesting much as you did towards the end of your pregnancy.

It's also a time when your baby is adjusting to life outside the womb, and you're getting to know your new baby and learning to be his parent and read his signals. Let's now look at some ways to make what can be a rough and intense time easier for you. This, in turn, will make it easier for your baby.

Tips to help you get through the early days on broken sleep.

- Mark your calendar for three months after the birth, and allow yourself, in that time, to take it easy, rest and focus on simply feeding your baby and yourself, and getting as much sleep as you can. Of course you won't be able to do this all the time. And you may feel thrilled that your pregnancy is over and ready to be out and about much sooner, especially if your baby turns out to be a good sleeper. But at least allow yourself to take it a bit easier in that first intense newborn stage – particularly if you don't have a great deal of family support around you, as many of us don't.

- Prepare ahead with some frozen meals, and perhaps get a regular online shopping order set up. Hire a cleaner, if your budget allows, or some extra help around the house, such as a post-natal nurse or night nurse. Allow others to help if they offer, with offers of food or just holding the baby so you can get a rest or a shower.

- Limit your obligations and don't feel bad for saying no to visitors, particularly those demanding ones who expect to be waited on while they hold the baby. It's natural for everyone around you to be excited about a new baby, and want to spend as much time as possible cuddling and holding the new addition. But keep visits short if you don't feel up to it, and if your baby doesn't like being handed around for hours (many find it stressful and it can lead to an unsettled night) then simply take your baby and retreat to your bedroom. There is plenty of time for everyone to get to know your baby in the months and years ahead, and you have to prioritise your own well-being, and that of your newborn, at this special time.

- Sleep when the baby sleeps. Hard to do, when it feels like the only time you have 'off', but try not to stay awake if you could be sleeping, whenever possible. In the evenings, having a warm bath and some skin-to-skin with your baby and then an hour or two of sleep. This will make a big difference to how you feel the next morning. Especially if it ends up being an unsettled night!

- Agree on a timetable with your partner about who does night time wake ups. If you fall asleep early, perhaps your partner can do the first wake-up feed of the night, so you will get a good four or five hours of sleep before the next one – express a bottle of milk if you are breastfeeding, or have him wake and bring the baby to you, then settle him outside of the bedroom so you can fall straight back to sleep. Sharing the broken sleep means that the burden isn't just on one person.

- Prioritise eating well. When you are exhausted it can be easy to fall into the habit of existing on toast and coffee. But you will need nutritious food to recover from the birth, and to keep your energy levels high. Have some cut-up fruit and vegetables close to hand, enjoy soup, yogurt, salad and other easy meals. Drink lots of water, and try and get some protein and healthy carbohydrates into your diet, too. Keep taking your pre-natal vitamins as you rest and recover from the birth, and don't drink too much coffee, as it can interfere with your sleep.

- Finally, remember that time spent with your baby is the most important thing right now, as she settles into the world and your bond grows. Give yourself lots of time to settle her. Ask visitors to make their own drinks rather than waiting on them hand and foot. And put your feet up as much as you can. You've just been through a huge physical and emotional life change, and you need to treat yourself accordingly!

Chapter 2 - Getting Organized

We now know what babies and toddlers should be doing when it comes to sleep. We know that newborns are naturally unsettled, and that there are things we can do to help them along as they learn how to sleep properly, such as getting some natural light in the daytime. And we know how to set up a safe sleeping area for the baby.

What we also need to understand is that there's no magic trick to create a perfect sleeper – sometimes you just get lucky, other times you have a fretful baby who struggles to fall and stay asleep. What you can do is educate yourself about how to encourage good sleep.

In this chapter we'll build on this knowledge and dive into how we can establish the right environment for good sleep. We'll learn about sleep associations, and how they can help your baby to get ready to drift off. And we'll also look at creating a sleep log, which can help you develop a better understanding of how your baby's sleep is changing over time. This can be helpful both for your own peace-of-mind, and also to show your GP or child health nurse, should you decide to seek further help with your baby's sleeping habits.

Everything You Need for Your Baby's Sleeping Area

- Sheets: Around six cot or bassinet sheets is perfect, and you can also use folded single-bed sheets if you need to. You can also put a pillowcase over a small mattress when your baby is very little.
- A mattress protector to put over the mattress will protect it from leaking bottles and nappies. Or use a blanket or a towel underneath the sheet.

- A mosquito net may be helpful in the warmer months, if you live in a mosquito-prone area. There is nothing worse than waking up to a miserable baby covered in mosquito bites.
- A cot or bassinet. A small bassinet is great for the first few months, but you can also put your baby in a cot from the start. Ideally you want something that's easy to move, and that allows you to access your baby easily, for example during night feeds and if you need to pat your baby to sleep.

Some cots come with two levels, so you can raise them when the baby is small then lower them once your baby is old enough to climb out of the cot.

When choosing a cot, look for smooth, rounded edges and no extra decorations such as beads, which can be hazardous. The cot should have high sides so your baby can't fall out once they are a bit older (ie two feet from the base of the mattress to the top of the cot sides). If it has drop-sides, they need to be childproof and work smoothly, and the mattress should fit the cot well. Your cot also needs to have no more than two to three inches between bars, so your baby can't fit his or her head through.

If you are buying a second-hand or vintage cot, be aware that old paint may contain lead. You'll need to strip or repaint the cot, if this is the case. Also ensure that any decorations on an old cot can't be pulled off, and that the cot is strong and sturdy.

- Babies tend to settle and sleep better on a dense, firm mattress, so look for these when you are shopping around. A good-quality clean, firm, second-hand mattress is fine – just leave it in the sun for a day or two to air it out.

- Cot bumpers (a soft piece of padded fabric that surrounds the inside of the cot) are no longer recommended by baby safety experts, as they can restrict air flow to the cot and also pose risks of suffocation or strangulation, should they come loose. There should be absolutely no extra fabric, pillows or soft toys around a sleeping baby. Children do not need pillows until they move into a toddler bed.

Do you need any additional safety products?

There is no substitute for planning your baby's sleeping environment and following the latest safety guidelines, remaining vigilant and using your common sense and instincts when it comes to keeping your baby safe while sleeping.

Having said that, a night light can be very helpful to cope with night feeds, and so you can move around without waking the baby too much. It can also be a comfort to your baby once they are older and wake in the middle of the night.

A sound monitor can be used if your baby's nap area is a long way away from your living room for day time naps. If your baby sleeps in your room for the first six month, you won't need it for night time – you'll hear him! However, sleep monitors don't monitor breathing, so can't be considered a safety device, and one downside is that they can be disruptive, as you will hear every noise your baby makes while sleeping.

Breathing monitors may be given to small or unwell babies, but are not generally used for all babies. They have an alarm that goes off if the baby stops breathing, but can also give frequent false alarms. I always recommend that all parents should know how to do heart-lung resuscitation, though, so you know what to do in an emergency.

Where Should Your Baby Sleep?

Ideally, for the first six months, your baby should sleep in your room for safety reasons. If, after this point, you decide you would like the baby in a separate room, the risk of SIDS (Sudden Infant Death Syndrome) drops, but it is still safer to have the baby in your room for the first six months, and as long as you like into the future. Refer to the first chapter for information about co-sleeping safely, or consider having a cot next to your bed so you can hear and reach your baby easily.

Sleep Associations: What They Are & How They Can Help

Sleep associations are essentially signals that make your baby feel sleepy. As adults, we develop them too – reading in bed before sleep, a warm bath, a particular time each night that we head for bed, and our pre-bed rituals such as brushing our teeth and putting on our pyjamas.

Setting up sleep associations for babies is much the same thing, and as your baby grows and you settle into living with him or her, you'll find a routine around sleep will help you to organise your days better and enjoy a well-rested, happy baby.

Read on for some ways you can create sleep associations and start to establish a routine with your baby.

Create a flexible daily routine

Strangely enough, your day time routine is itself a powerful sleep association. Research shows that if your baby is part of your daily routine, he or she will develop mature circadian rhythms more quickly, and thus sleep better at night. In other words, take your baby with you on your daily activities so you are active and quiet at the same times. Studies on infants have shown that regular exposure to daylight will help your baby adapt to the cycle of day and night. It's also been shown that babies exposed to light in the afternoon will sleep better.

A daily routine may look something like this:

- Wake up. Give your baby a feed, then get dressed and head outside, weather permitting, to the playground or shops so you have some daylight and fresh air. Some 'play' in the form of eye contact, singing and chatting to your baby will also stimulate them and ready them for a good sleep later on. Activities such as baby swimming lessons or a children's session at a local library are other ways to fill your morning.

  Tummy time is great for giving your baby some exercise and strengthening his neck and shoulders, and can be done on a soft rug from birth. Some babies love it, others hate it, but if you build up gradually to around 15 minutes a day it's a great first workout for your baby and will help to tire him out. Tummy time should always be done under supervision – hold a toy in front of your baby's face to keep them happy as they work out.

- Home for a morning nap
  With a very young baby, this will be only an hour or two after waking. For older babies and toddlers, it might be after lunch. You will know your baby is tired as they will start to complain and perhaps cry, avoid eye contact, and start to rub their eyes or clench their fists. Each baby has their own 'tired' signs, and you will soon start to recognise yours.

- Wake up
  Now it's time for lunch, play time, and try to get outside for a walk and some more daylight. Board books, singing, movement and chatter are other good ways to give your baby the stimulation she needs to learn and grow.

- Afternoon nap
  With very young babies, there is not much point trying to predict nap times as they aren't established straight away, and will change from day to day at first. But older babies will start to fall asleep reliably in the afternoon for a longer nap. Ideally, they should be awake again by three, or four at the latest, if you want them to be in bed again for 7.30pm, but this is up to the individual baby.

Some babies can be up at five and asleep again by six; others will be up until 10pm if they are asleep past four pm. You will need to track your own babies sleep to work out when and how much sleep they need – we will cover sleep logs in a later chapter.

- Evening routine and bedtime
  Creating a predictable bedtime routine is key to establishing good sleep habits and making sleep training run more smoothly later on. Start with dinner, or a feed, followed by a warm bath, perhaps a massage, and then quiet time before bed with lots of cuddles, singing, a top-up feed and maybe a board book or two, then lights out at the same time each evening. Busy days with lots of attention, chatter and cuddles for your baby will "fill their cup" so they are more ready for sleep at night, too.

Please note that you don't have to live by this routine – depending on your own nature, you might prefer more flexibility. But with babies, a flexible, yet predictable routine can provide structure and security for your little one, and help you feel more in control, too.

Create a strong sense of night time being sleep time

Helping your baby understand that night time is for sleeping is crucial for establishing a good sleep routine. At night, after dinner, a warm bath can help to make your baby ready for sleep. Doing the same things before bed each night – a story, some quiet time in their sleeping room – will also ready them for sleep.

Throughout the night, too, make sure that wake times are as quiet and boring as possible to convey to you baby that *there's nothing happening here, it's time to sleep.* Minimise eye contact, and don't have any play or bright lights or screens on during night feeds or wakings (this another reason a night light can be useful).

Try not to move your baby too much if you are feeding them, as this will help them to stay drowsy. An open-sided cot bed next to yours will help you deal with night wakings with as little disruption as possible. If you need a light to see what you're doing, choose a very low wattage so the room remains as dark as possible. Black-out blinds on the windows can also help to keep your baby from waking too much during the night.

Introduce wind-down time at night, and try to stick to it

Even if you aren't following a strict routine, it's a good idea to give your baby plenty of time to wind down at night. Think of your own night time routine and how it's easier to get to sleep if you've carried out familiar rituals beforehand, such as putting on your night clothes, and brushing your teeth and maybe reading a book. Your baby will respond to sleep cues, too – it's just a matter of finding ones that work for you. These could include the following:

- A warm bath, perhaps with some lavender oil added.
- A massage in a warm, dimly lit room, with soothing oils. A bedtime massage has been shown to improve baby sleep.
- A bedtime story or two – simple board books will do. It's not so much the 'reading' but the cuddling in bed, the calming reading voice, and the familiarity of the ritual that will settle your baby.
- Skin to skin contact for very small babies, who may like to be tucked up against you in bed to fall asleep.
- A bedtime song such as Twinkle Twinkle Little Star.
- A soft, soothing stroke of the back or hand, although not all babies will like this and it may actually wake some up – you'll need to test it yourself!
- Feeding your baby right before sleep, then putting them down and waiting until they drop off, is also a way to help them fall easily into sleep.
- Feeding your baby to sleep is also an option chosen by many mothers, including me. Eventually you need to break the association with feeding and sleep, but when the time is right, it will happen. We will get to that later!
- If you don't want to get into the habit of feeding your baby to sleep, you can feed her until she is drowsy, perhaps already dressed in her sleeping bag, then settle her in her cot so that she drops off on her own, knowing you are close by but not 'needing' you to fall asleep. This will teach her that she can put herself to sleep, and may make things easier in the long run. As with everything, though, you will need to work out what your particular baby prefers and go along with that, to some extent. More highly strung or clingy babies may resist being

put down in their cot to sleep and will only fall asleep in your arms – there's nothing wrong with this, particularly in the early days, so don't let anyone tell you you're "creating a rod for your own back" – everything can be changed when the time is right.

Ensure the temperature is right

An overheated room isn't great for sleep quality or for safety. Body temperature changes throughout the day, and once we fall asleep it naturally drops. Ensuring your baby's body temperature drops off at bedtime will encourage a deeper sleep, and can also help them fall asleep faster. If the temperature is too hot or cold, the baby's body will try to regulate it, and it will take longer for sleep to descend.

The ideal temperature is between 68 and 72 degrees Fahrenheit (or 19 to 21 degrees Celsius.) If it's hard for you to achieve this in your house, dressing the baby suitably is the next best option. As I have already mentioned, sleeping bags that your baby wears are the safest and most reliable option for good sleep – you can buy them in varying tog thicknesses to suit your particular climate and time of year. Generally, go for a thick tog in winter, a thin one in summer, and dress your baby in a sleepsuit underneath that covers his or her feet. You will soon work out what's best for your baby, and if they are overdressed they will look red and fretful, and feel hot to the touch. If your baby's chest or belly feel sweaty, remove a layer of clothing or dial down the heating.

The right temperature is also essential for safety. The risk of Sudden Infant Death Syndrome, or SIDS, increases in winter when babies might be bundled up under too many blankets and overheat.

Create darkness

As with all people, babies cycle between periods of wakefulness and rest, but unlike adults, they have no way of controlling this for themselves. When they get overstimulated and tired, they need to transition into an environment of low stimulation so they can fall asleep. One of the best ways of doing this is to create a room that is very dark. This is easy at night, and in the daytime you can achieve it with a blackout blind that can be placed over your window with plastic suction cups. As soon as your baby sees the dark room they will begin to anticipate sleep, their muscles will relax, and they will begin to feel drowsy. And indeed at any time of day when your baby gets upset or overstimulated, taking them to a quiet, dim room will help to calm them down.

Minimise noise and use white noise, if necessary

As with bright light, too much noise can be overwhelming for babies, who will become overstimulated and find it even harder to drop off. Obviously you can't create a perfectly soundless environment, but you can use white noise within your baby's sleeping area to block out other sounds.

White noise can reduce stress, encourage deeper sleep, and reduce any overstimulation. You can buy white noise generating machines, or use an app on your smartphone. It's important, though, that the white noise isn't too loud (no more than 50 to 60 decibels), or too close to the crib. And while it can be helpful for some babies, it may not work for all of them. But it's worth a try! If you want to phase it out eventually, you can just dial it down a little each day until it's off.

A table or ceiling fan is another sleep aid that can be helpful, both for the monotonous sound and for the air movement, which can promote a restful sleep.

What is a Sleep Log?

Some parents like to track their baby's sleep on a sleep log. This can be as simple as a notebook, or you can use an Excel spreadsheet or even an app to record your baby's sleep. Logging the length and timing of your baby's night sleeps and naps may help you identify a pattern to their sleep, and keep track of just how many hours of rest they are getting. This may be useful to show your child health nurse, or to simply get a better understanding of your child's need for sleep.

You will also be able to note changes over a longer period of time, and perhaps get some comfort from the fact that your baby's sleep is gradually improving. And a sleep log may also help you work out just how much sleep your baby needs to be happy and alert during the daytime, if you look back a day or two and note just how much sleep they have (or haven't) had, and compare it with their behaviour.

Sometimes, paying attention to their sleep can solve certain problems. For example, my son would go to bed at night easily as long as he was awake from his afternoon nap by no later than 3pm. Any later than that, and he would be up until 10pm. So I would always aim to have him down for his nap by 1.30pm, and around 3pm I would start gently making a little noise and allowing him to wake up. Once you work out how your child's sleep works best, you can plan around your 'best practice' findings accordingly.

While a sleep log won't work for everyone, it's useful to keep track of your baby's sleeping patterns, and will help you feel more in control, too. There are even shareable online apps that you can use to log naps and other information, which you can share with other caregivers looking after your child.

Chapter 3 - Baby Sleep Problems

8 Common Baby Sleep Problems by Age & How to Manage Them

Newborns and small babies

At this age, you have to accept a degree of disrupted sleep. It will pass, but my best advice is to give yourself a break. As I've said earlier, take all the help you are offered, don't give yourself a hard time about a messy house or a takeaway dinner, and know that it will soon be over and everyone will be sleeping better. Just rest, enjoy your newborn and recover from the birth and pregnancy. It's honestly not for long. Having said that, there are a few sleep issues you may come up against that you may want to address for safety reasons or just because they will make your life easier and aren't difficult to fix.

- Not being able to sleep on their back

At this age, it's recommended that babies are always put to bed on their backs, as any other position increases the risk of SIDS. One solution is to swaddle babies firmly in a blanket to help them feel more secure and stop them flailing around. Another is to rock them gently to sleep, then move them into their bassinet or cot once they are deeply asleep. If you are consistent, she will eventually get used to sleeping on her back.

- Not knowing the difference between night and day

As we have discussed, babies have no sense of night or day, and wake frequently throughout the night to feed. We've looked at ways you can start to give them a sense of night and day, which will help over time. These include going outside and getting some natural light in the daytime, and keeping nighttime wakings as dark and quiet as you can, so she gets the message that darkness is for sleeping.

- Hunger

If you are breastfeeding, be sure to keep in touch with a lactation consultant to ensure that your baby is getting a good feed, as a hungry baby will find it hard to sleep. Breastfeeding can take a while to establish, so in those early days you may need to hold your baby or feed for a long time to get them off to sleep. Always get as much help as you need and you can look forward to better sleep once the feeding routine is established.

With bottle-fed babies, again, ensure that the baby is getting enough food, checking the instructions for mixing the formula up carefully. A warm bath, followed by a feed, should ensure a good sleep.

Two to three month old babies

- Sleep regression

Around this age your baby should be sleeping better, however you may also notice a sleep regression. This often accompanies a growth spurt or development leap, and is characterised by an alert, active baby who shows no signs of wanting to sleep. There's not much you can do apart from work on solidifying your night time routine – bath, story, bed – so that your baby gets the message that nights are for sleeping, not playing. It will soon pass, but if it's exhausting you, see if you can get some extra rest or naps in the meantime. We will look more at sleep regressions later on.

Feeding through the night is another habit you can fall in to, especially with breastfed babies. Your baby feeds little and often, leaving you exhausted. If you keep your baby in your room with you, you may be able to manage night feeds without fully waking up. But if you would like to stretch out the time between feeds so you get more sleep, try and give your baby a really good feed last thing at night, and perhaps express a bottle of milk so your partner can take over one feed (although this may be more hassle than it's worth, and some breastfed babies will simply refuse a bottle and hold out for the breast. Creating set times for bottles or breastfeeds in the daytime and trying to stick to them may also guide your baby towards a more regular sleeping and feeding pattern through the might.

- Teething pain

Some babies may seem unsettled when they have a tooth coming through, with red cheeks and drooling. Extra cuddles, a teething ring and a warm bath will all help to settle him. Teething will generally pass quickly, but if your baby seems to be particularly unhappy, a visit to your family doctor is worth a try, as they may recommend some baby painkillers which will help with sleep, too. Having said that, teething can also be used as a catch-all term for any unsettled behaviour – sometimes, it's worth looking a little deeper to find out if there's any other solutions to usettled behaviour.

Four to five month old babies

- Overstimulation

Around this age your baby may drop a nap, and start sleeping less in the daytime. This may lead to her being overtired at night and harder to settle. It's important to realise that an overtired baby may 'fire up' and become much more active, loud and energetic, rather than sleepy. This can be a sign of overstimulation, so if your baby seems overtired, try starting the bedtime routine a little earlier with all its associated sleep cues so they can catch up on sleep.

My second son used to "flap" himself to sleep, discharging extra energy by pumping his arms up and down. Even now, at six, he will do a bit of gymnastics before bed. It doesn't mean he isn't ready for bed, though, so I will firmly guide him to his bed at the right time and he will fall asleep within minutes. Babies and children often fight sleep – but don't let them win!

Sometimes, with an overtired baby, it takes longer for them to wind down, which can create a vicious circle of another late night followed by another unsettled day. It may help to 'break the cycle' with a busy afternoon that includes some play and outside time, followed by a good feed, a long bath and an early bedtime. No matter how alert your baby seems, keep in mind ideal sleep quantities for each age bracket and aim to get them – very tired children won't learn and thrive as well as well-rested ones.

Six months

- Still waking up wanting a feed

Although we don't remember it in the morning, we all wake up during the night a couple of times, and fall back to sleep again almost immediately with no memory of the event. Babies need to learn to fall back to sleep as well, preferably on their own and without requiring too much help from their caregivers, past the age of about six months.

If you've been feeding your baby to sleep, you might now consider moving this feed to thirty minutes before bedtime, and following it with a board book story and some lullabies in bed. You can expect some fussing at this change of routine, but if you are consistent, she will drift off without the bottle or breast if she is tired. This will hopefully also make night wakings easier – if she learns that she can get back to sleep without a feed, just your voice and perhaps a gentle stroke should be enough to settle her again.

Of course, if you don't mind feeding through the night, don't feel you have to do this. But if you are exhausted during the day, it might be a good idea to introduce some gentle sleep training around six months to make day-to-day life easier. There will be much more on this later!

- Early waking

Some babies wake early, raring to go. You can try adjusting naps and bedtimes, or put a black-out blind over the window to try and push her wake up time back a little. Another option is to bring her into your bed and hope that she drifts back to sleep.

Ultimately, though, early mornings are part and parcel of having a young baby, so getting to bed earlier yourself so you can handle the early start may be the best solution.

Fixing Less Common Reasons for Poor Sleep

Sickness

Unfortunately sickness – an upset tummy, an earache, a cold – can all result in terrible sleep. Keep on hand a baby painkiller recommended by your doctor or child health nurse so you can administer it when pain strikes in the middle of the night. Hopefully, the illness will pass quickly and sleep will return. But when this happens, you may have to simply accept a disrupted night and hope for some respite the following day. We will cover more on handling sleep problems caused by sickness later on.

Travel or a change of routine

Even now that my kids are older, I accept that the first night in a new place is going to be difficult. A change of routine, the excitement of a new environment and possibly a long nap on the journey will all result in a bad night's sleep, or a late, drawn-out bedtime. However, by the second night, everyone should be exhausted and sleep well.

Travel with babies can be difficult for this and many other reasons, so my suggestion is to manage your expectations and take things easy. Travelling with children does get easier as they get older, and more fun, particularly once everyone can read and swim. But in the early days, it's not always relaxing or even worth the hassle, a lot of the time.

At these times, if you have some kind of a routine or structure that is familiar to your baby – such as a warm bath, followed by stories in bed – you can always return to this to give your child the signal that it's time to sleep. Extra cuddles and lots of reassurance will also help.

At times of disruption – travel, growth spurts, developmental leaps – a familiar routine is a great way to keep things on track until everyone adjusts to the new reality.

A new caregiver or starting daycare are other things that can cause your baby to be unsettled and fussy, often just when you need them to be 'good.' Remember, your baby isn't trying to make your life harder, they are just unsettled and need you to show them that everything is fine.

Personally, I have always been a huge fan of stories in bed with my babies and young children. It is a nice way to unwind together at the end of the day, and as your child grows it will help them with talking and learning about the world and using their imagination. Plus, reading to your children will set them up very well for school later on – any time you give it now will pay off later.

Only sleeping while being held

This is a tricky one, and some trial-and-error is required if you want to break this habit. Often, introducing a white noise CD while rocking or holding your baby will give her another sleep cue. After a few days, you can try putting her down while playing the white noise, gently patting, rocking or shushing until she is asleep.

Sometimes babies need to know you are there to fall asleep. So if you are trying this, stay with your baby until he is deeply asleep. Shush, pat, rock – do anything apart from lie down with your baby or pick him up. He may object, but will soon learn that he can fall asleep without being held, as long as he knows you are there. Once he has taught himself to drift off, you will be able to leave the room earlier without too much trouble.

An overtired baby that finds it hard to get to sleep

If you get to know your baby's signs of tiredness – rubbing eyes, grizzling, sometimes clenched fists – you will know to put them down at the first sign, if you can, before they get really exhausted and overtired. Sometimes, though, you miss that magic moment and it becomes harder to get your baby to sleep as they are so worked up. Sometimes, a pram or a car drive can help as the movement lulls them to sleep. Or staying with them in a dark room until they drop off is another way to break through the overtiredness and allow sleep to arrive.

Only catnapping for short periods of time

Some babies will only sleep for twenty minutes then wake up again, still seeming tired. In this case, go back to basics and look at your whole sleep routine and environment. Is the room dark, quiet and the right temperature? Are you putting her down soon enough? Putting a baby down to sleep when they are already overtired can make it harder for them to reach a deep sleep. Also, look at your nighttime routine – are you following a set pattern each night, with afternoon play and daylight, a good feed, long bath and set bedtime? Putting in place a firmer structure can help some babies adjust and sleep better.

Sometimes, though, it's just a matter of getting through until they learn to sleep better, and if this is the case, you may need to look at ways to cope with less sleep, which we looked at earlier one.

Falling asleep in the car or the pram

With some babies, they may fall asleep while you are out, and you'll find that when you get home and attempt to put them into bed, they wake up again, missing their nap. If this happens to you, it may be easier to not disturb them once they are asleep. If they are in a pram, simply wheel it somewhere quiet and keep an eye on it until they wake up. If you are in a car, park somewhere shady and pull out a book or your smartphone, keeping the air-conditioning or heating on depending on the weather. If you take snacks and drinks with you when you are out, you can simply enjoy nap time in your car. But never, ever leave a sleeping baby in a car unattended.

What Your Baby's Sleep Habits Mean

If your baby finds it hard to fall asleep

They may be overtired or unsettled for some reason. In this case, it's often good to start bedtime earlier, and see if that helps. An overtired baby will find it much harder to get to sleep.

They may be hungry. Around six months, when your baby starts eating solids, they may suddenly start to sleep much more deeply. You can also try introducing high-fat, dense foods to satisfy their hunger. Toast with lots of avocado and butter, for example, is a dense, high-fat food that will fill your baby up. Another good food is pureed chicken soup – the protein is very filling.

They may be having a growth spurt or developmental leap, or unsettled for some other reason. More on this later.

Unexplained unsettled behaviour

Unfortunately, there is never a 'one size fits all' solution when it comes to baby behaviour. Nor is there a set of guidelines that will solve all of your sleep problems. What you can do is understand what is normal behaviour and also keep in mind that the tricky phases will pass with time. Sometimes, just ensuring you get enough downtime by cutting back on other activities if you are feeling worn out is the best solution. Whatever your baby is struggling with usually won't last for long, and as time goes by your sleep will return.

Other strange sleep habits

Snorting and snoring

Babies make all sorts of funny noises, and snorting or snoring during sleep is nothing to be concerned about. Babies may also snore gently when they have a blocked nose. A vaporiser or humidifier in the room, or sitting with your baby in a steamy bathroom, may help to clear their nasal passages and make them more comfortable before sleep. Having said that, a baby who snores all the time, not just when under-the-weather, is worth seeing your doctor about, as it may be a sign of a health problem. Your doctor may refer you to a paediatric ear, nose and throat specialist for further tests.

Heavy sweating during sleep

Some babies tend to 'run hot', and you will notice that they sweat a lot while sleeping, particularly during their deep sleep and sometimes soaking their sheets. Because babies spend 50 per cent of their sleep time in deep sleep, if they sweat during this time, it will tend to be more noticeable. Always check the temperature of the room and ensure your baby is not overdressed, as overheating can be a risk factor for SIDS.

You should also mention excessive sweating to your doctor, as it can be a sign of an underlying health issue. Don't feel you have to pile your baby with blankets – they will let you know if they are cold, and you can also check how warm they are by feeling their hands or chest.

Of course, babies can also simply get very hot in summer. If you're hot, your baby probably is too. A warm, but not hot, bath and perhaps a clean wet flannel to suck on in the bath can ensure your baby stays cool and hydrated enough to drift off to sleep. But if the house feels cool and your baby is not overdressed yet still feels very hot, talk to your doctor.

Rocking and headbanging

Babies may sometimes get on all fours and rock in bed. It looks strange, but it's totally normal, particularly when they are drifting off to sleep. Babies also sometimes practise new physical movements while half asleep, again and again, until they finally lie down and sleep. Keep an eye on your baby if they are doing this in bed – it's quite fascinating! – but don't worry too much. It may be accompanied by head banging or rolling – again, weird, but totally normal. This often happens around six to nine months, when babies start to master new skills around movement and crawling.

Head banging may also be a distraction from the pain of a tooth coming in, and can continue for some time. It's rarely a sign of anything serious, but it's worth mentioning it to your doctor, especially if your child is showing any other signs of developmental delay.

Teeth grinding

Many babies grind their teeth, especially during sleep. It's also common when the first tooth comes through. It sounds awful, but isn't anything to worry about. You can, however, mention it when you take your baby to her first dental appointment, at around one year of age.

Chapter 4 - Preparing for Sleep Training

Sleep training is something that you might want to consider when you and your baby are both ready, if you feel desperate for sleep and want your baby to learn to drift off to sleep on her own. While it doesn't work for all babies (or parents), I believe that it's a reasonable approach that can have a positive impact on family life. Yes, there might be a few days of crying and broken sleep, but an exhausted parent who is waking every few hours to pat, rock and feed a baby is not ideal in the long-term, either, particularly if it's affecting your mental health, happiness levels, work and relationships.

Bear in mind, though, that you don't have to sleep train if you don't want to. If you can live with broken sleep, and find ways to manage, such as co-sleeping or napping when your baby naps, you don't need to do anything. It's up to you, and you should always do what feels right.

If you don't want to sleep train, simply continue with your bedtime routine and other strategies for night waking we have already outlined, and work around it until your baby is sleeping better, or you decide that the time is right for sleep training. You might choose to keep the baby's cot next to your bed, or place a mattress in the baby's room, or alternate 'on duty' nights with your partner until your baby is better at getting through the night without waking.

Ultimately, as with everything to do with looking after a baby, you can look at the research and current information, take what you can and decide what will work for you and your family. Before we dive into the nitty-gritty of sleep training, though, we need to look at what it is. We'll also cover how to work out if your baby is ready for sleep training, and how to choose the right sleep training method for your baby.

Hard Truths about Sleep Training that All Parents Must Know

Sleep training, sometimes (wrongly) referred to as 'crying it out', is essentially teaching your baby how to fall asleep on their own, or with limited help.

You can go in to the room periodically to provide reassurance – patting, stroking and soothing – but you don't pick the baby up or take him into your bed. The aim is to 'train' your baby to fall asleep independently, without all the rocking, cuddling, bottles, breastfeeding and other sleep aids you have been using.

It can be a divisive issue. Some people believe that you should never leave a baby to cry, that you will do untold psychological damage, and that you should simply go along with what the baby wants. Child development experts don't always agree on whether it's an appropriate solution to poor sleep. But what we do know is that it's possible to introduce some sleep training in a gentle way, without simply closing the door on your baby and leaving them alone until morning. In the old days that was known as the 'crying it out' method, and we have definitely moved on from that! Here are some things you need to consider when deciding to sleep train.

Sleep training doesn't always work

Whether you follow the old-fashioned (and no longer recommended) path of leaving your baby alone until morning, or try a more gentle approach, be aware that success is not guaranteed. Both methods work with some babies, but not all of them. Some will put up more of a fight, and you may have to accept this and remind yourself that in a few years they will be in their own beds and sleeping well. And that when they are teenagers you will struggle to stop them from sleeping at all, and you will perhaps long for their baby days!

Bear in mind, too, that for around 20 per cent of babies, sleep training simply doesn't work – they may be too young, or not able to cope with separation from their parents. Like so many parenting scenarios, it comes down to your child's unique temperament. And yours, too – you may find that you can't cope with the sound of your baby screaming for you in distress, and abandon the idea on the very first night.

It's not something you need to beat yourself up about

Some parents find it incredibly hard to make the decision to sleep train, worrying that they are being cruel or causing their baby long-lasting emotional damage. What you need to keep in mind, though, is that in the setting of a loving, safe family environment, sleep training is unlikely to do any lasting damage. And in fact, if you are returning to work, looking after other children or driving regularly, it's essential for you to get a good nights' sleep too, for safety reasons and for your own mental health and wellbeing. So please don't beat yourself up about wanting to change your baby's sleep habits. Sometimes, for the good of the wider family, it's worth at least trying.

Bear in mind, too, that once upon a time, parents had much more family support to draw on, with grandparents and other family members stepping up to help with childcare and quietly appear in the small hours to give exhausted parents a break. Plus, these days, many women combine work with childcare, so need to be alert and busy during the day.

Today's families also tend to be much smaller and more contained, and nearby family help or help from older siblings is not always available. What this means is that problems with sleep fall squarely on the parents' shoulders (often the mother's). It's not unreasonable, in today's pressured parenting environment, to work towards a good night's sleep!

It's a good idea to address sleeping problems sooner rather than later

With babies and children, the longer you leave a particular behaviour unaddressed – whether that be thumb sucking or falling asleep in front of the TV – the harder it is to eventually change it. So if you lie down with your baby every night, or feed them to sleep, they will get used to it and not want to change. If you don't mind, it's fine – you don't need to change anything. But if you want to spend less time at night on bedtimes, for example, you're better off addressing it head on rather than waiting and hoping that things will change by themselves. Chances are, if the baby likes it (and if it means being close to you, they will) they won't change without a bit of a struggle. There will be some pain and crying while you put in place the new habits, but if you are firm, consistent and determined, the pain will be short lived and you can look forward to everyone having better sleep and your evenings back. As a parent, you are in charge, and if you are consistent, your child will come to the party eventually. They want to please you, after all.

There is no set formula that is guaranteed to work

Some sleep training books will offer a very structured approach to sleep training, but what you need to remember is that the authors don't know your or your baby. So what works for some babies won't work for others – and it doesn't mean you're doing anything wrong. What you need to look for is what some researchers call the 'magic moment' when your baby will stop crying and gradually drift off to sleep. This may be due to lots of reassurance and visits from parents, or your baby may do better if you remove yourself from the room for a little longer between visits.

You will work this out yourself, and you may be surprised to discover that your baby needs a bit of time to do some 'unwinding' crying on their own, knowing you are nearby, in order to get to sleep.

Even now, my pre-schooler son will often fall asleep faster if I leave him alone, even though he may call for me. If I go in, he wants to chat and engage with me, and the whole process takes longer. Eventually, you will work out what helps your particular baby. You'll also be able to tell the difference between a falling-asleep, not particularly distressed cry that is simply the baby unwinding and releasing pent-up stress before sleep, and a seriously distressed, anxious cry that is not going to result in sleep any time soon.

It's important to remember, too, that some crying in babies, toddlers, children and even adults is healthy. A good cry relaxes us and discharges emotions and tensions, so don't feel that you are doing your child any harm if they are left to cry a little. Sometimes, it's simply part of their falling-asleep process, and helps them to relax and wind down. It's only a problem if you leave them to cry alone for hours, or ignore any serious distress. A calm, relaxed approach, with some gentle words of support, is the best way to handle sleep training.

What you definitely don't want to do is to try sleep training, abandon it, then try again, on and off for an indefinite period of time. This is unfair on your baby, as they don't know what you want from them and they won't know what to expect from bedtimes.

Your baby may sleep better after training, but there will still be bad nights

Sleep training isn't a miracle solution, and it's not about solving all of your baby's sleep problems for ever. It's more about improving matters so that ideally your baby can drift off to sleep independently, and you feel more rested in general.

You will still have nights when your baby needs you – perhaps they had a bad day, feel unwell, or they are going through a growth spurt or developmental leap and need some extra reassurance. There's no harm in going to your baby in the night when they cry out for you – that is simply part of being a parent. It doesn't mean you need to pick her up or bring her into your bed, though, unless you want to. Once you've done some basic sleep training, your baby should generally be able to get back to sleep with a few gentle words and a reassuring stroke from you. And if you have an unsettled night due to sickness or some other reason, return to your routine as soon as possible so you don't undo all the progress you've made.

In summary, it's up to you – and in the context of a loving home, many child health experts believe that some gentle sleep training is worth a try if you are feeling exhausted and irritable.

Is Your Baby Ready for Sleep Training?

Around six months is a good time to think about whether your baby is ready for sleep training. Before this time, it's developmentally appropriate for your baby to be waking in the night for a feed, and they can't really be 'trained' to sleep for longer. But if you decide you want to try and change things, don't wait for too long after this point, and sleep habits will be more established and harder to break.

By six months of age, a baby will be used to you picking them up and rocking them back to sleep, and perhaps feeding them, too. But if you feel you would like more sleep, then there is nothing wrong with trying to change things a little. So if at this point you decide you would like to try sleep training, it may be that over a period of three or four nights of some crying, you will find that your baby is settling and sleeping much better.

So when is sleep training recommended? Read on for some common reasons to try sleep training.

If your baby is waking through the night to be fed.

Here, you may not mind feeding your baby through the night. There's nothing wrong with doing so, particularly if you are breastfeeding and your baby is close by, and you can feed without either of you waking up too much. But if you are still waking through the night to heat bottles and your baby requires soothing and rocking to get back to sleep, it's not unreasonable to at least try to change things at this point.

Around six months is a good time to try this – your baby is likely to be much more settled and relaxed, and you have gotten past the initial shock of a new baby. If you feel you'd like to push for a bit more routine around sleep, give it a go.

If your baby is unable to drift off to sleep alone

Again, this may not be a problem for you. But if you have other children to look after, or you simply want your evenings back and would like your baby to be able to fall asleep independently, trying some gentle sleep training may be a good idea. Single parents and parents of twins may also need to try sleep training sooner for practical reasons.

As your baby gets bigger, rocking to sleep can become harder, so you may find that your aching arms make the decision for you! The end result will ideally be that you carry out your usual bedtime routine, as we discussed in earlier chapters, settle your baby in bed, and he or she falls asleep independently, perhaps with a little 'wind-down' crying. And you get your evenings back!

If your baby is sleeping longer at night already

Once your baby is bigger, and eating three meals a day, and sleeping well at night, you may consider sleep training to move your baby into better long-term sleep habits. If waking up to breastfeed or have a bottle in the middle of the night is no longer necessary from a nutritional point of view, but seems more like a habit, you may choose to train now.

If your baby shows some ability to self soothe

If your baby seems relaxed in general, and falls asleep easily without seeming fretful or distressed, you may want to try sleep training now. Some babies are temperamentally more highly strung than others, but if you feel like your baby will respond well to sleep training, and you are generally happy with her development, there's no harm in giving it a go at six months of age. You can always try again at nine or twelve months if it doesn't work. If you're really lucky, you might end up with a baby who prefers to drift off to sleep without any extra attention. Though if that's the case, you probably won't be reading this book!

The timing is right for your family

Addressing disrupted nights and trying to get your whole family sleeping better is going to take a few nights of disruption, effort and willpower on your behalf. Factor this in, read up on sleep training, and plan your approach and time so that you have the best chance of success. Don't sleep train when you are busy at work or with other activities and need your rest. Make sure you don't have other things on, such as visitors coming to stay or a holiday away from your home and routine. Nor should you attempt to sleep train when your baby is sick or otherwise unsettled with some new change in his routine, such as starting at a new daycare.

Choose a time when everyone is well and happy, and you can give it your full focus for a few nights. If it doesn't work, so be it. You can always try again in a few months time.

How to Choose the Right Sleep Training Method for Your Baby

There is no one sleep training method that is guaranteed to work. Research shows that they all achieve around the same degree of success, but it will depend on what works best for your child and his particular temperament. The most important thing is to be consistent. The four main methods are "Cry it Out", "Fade Out", "Pick up Put Down" and "Camping Out."

And there's the final method, that you may find, eventually, is that the best thing for you and your family is to co-sleep with your baby, because he or she demands to be close – up to you. You can always try sleep training again later.

As I've mentioned, by the time your baby is around six months old, you'll have some idea of his temperament. In fact, you'll get a sense of his personality as soon as you meet him, but by six months you should know whether he's a fretful, clingy baby or a more relaxed one. Does he need to be close at all times or is he happy for periods alone? Is he determined to always have his own way, or does he show some flexibility? All of these factors will help you decide what kind of sleep training to use.

The first thing to work out is if you need to sleep train at all. If you are lucky, you may have a baby that can naturally self-soothe. Try this test: put your tired, well-fed baby to sleep and let him cry for a little while. He may drop off to sleep quickly all by himself, in which case you don't need to sleep train at all – lucky you!

But it's not always so easy. Generally speaking, a very sensitive, highly strung child will need a slower approach, or may not cope with sleep training at all.

A more strong-willed child may need a firmer approach, and be left to fall asleep largely on his own with a few nights of crying, because a parent coming into the room will strengthen his resolve to fight back against the new system!

Other, relatively easy-going babies often respond well to more gentle "No Cry", "Fading Out", or modified cry-it-out methods.

You also need to think about your own temperament: do you have the resolve for a fast, cry it out sleep training programme over a short period of time, or do you feel more comfortable taking longer to sleep train, but doing it more gently? Sleep training can be particularly hard when you are already sleep deprived, and for any parent, the sound of a crying baby is quite unbearable.

Plus, you need to think about other people in the family. Will children be woken by late-night screaming? Do you have a partner who can help share the burden of sleep training? You are looking at a minimum of three nights of disruption, with many babies taking seven to 10 nights before they are fully on board. So plan your strategy accordingly.

Ready to dive in?

In the next chapter, we'll give you a range of sleep training methods to try, from gentle training to faster methods that you carry out over several nights. We'll also look at what you need to do to succeed, and what happens if it doesn't work.

Chapter 5 - Sleep Training Success

4 Transformative Sleep Training Methods

Before we dive into the various sleep training methods, it's important to understand that there are no guarantees. And, as with everything to do with babies, there is no one answer. What you may end up using is a combination of the methods described below. You may find, once you start, that even two minutes of crying is unbearable for you, and choose to opt for a more gentle method. Always follow your own instincts here, and never do anything that makes you feel bad. But also try not to feel guilty about a bit of crying. It honestly won't do your baby any permanent damage. Permanent harm to children comes from things like abuse, war, food shortages and homelessness. So remember to keep the issue of sleep training in perspective!

It's developmentally normal for babies to cry before sleep – it helps them to discharge stress and tire themselves out, and you are not a 'bad parent' if you decide to try and get more sleep or help them fall asleep on their own. Remind yourself of the overall benefits of everyone getting more sleep, and also that famous parenting manta, "This too shall pass." An exhausted parent is not good for her baby either, and if you are returning to work or have other commitments, such as other children, it's perfectly reasonable to try and get your baby into better sleep habits.

Before you start, remember to implement a semi-regular day routine, with enough interesting and varied activity that your baby is left tired but not completely exhausted. Try and incorporate a walk or outing, some daylight, some 'play', a visit to a new house or relative, and lots of chatter and singing, etc, as well as three healthy and filling meals.

Naps should be regular and ideally not too late, as if your baby is overtired he will find it harder to settle.

This busy day can be followed by a set sequence of pre-bed rituals, as mentioned earier – a warm bath, perhaps a massage with some lavender-infused baby oil, a board-book story or two, a lullaby, lots of cuddles, and zipping your baby into his sleepsuit. Keep the lights low, turn the TV off, and make sure there is nothing interesting happening in another room that your baby will pick up on and want to investigate!

All of these rituals will send the message to your baby that it's time to relax and sleep, and make sleep training run more smoothly. If you have been feeding your baby to sleep, you can try breaking this association by feeding before stories and sleepsuit, rather than at the end. Keep calm yourself throughout the bedtime ritual, even if you are desperate to get the baby to sleep so you can have some time to yourself. Your baby will always pick up on your mood, so if you seem agitated or impatient, it may take longer to get him drowsy and drifting off.

Essentially, get your daytime house in order, including daytime naps and a bedtime ritual, before you try and tackle nights. We will cover naps more in an upcoming chapter.

OK – let's now move on to the four most common sleep training methods, and the benefits of each.

Fading out method

This has a number of names, but I'm calling it the Fading Method here. Essentially, with this method, you put your baby down to sleep after his normal bedtime ritual, and leave the room. At this point your baby will usually cry for you, but rather than go in immediately, you wait for a minute or so, before going back in to soothe, reassure and say a few gentle words. But you do not pick up your baby.

Gradually, you increase the amount of time you are out of the room, stretching it by a minute or two, until you are out of the room for 10-15 minute at a time. Ideally, your baby tires himself out and drifts off to sleep. If this method is going to work, it should do so within a week. Some people find that this method distresses the baby more, as every time you reappear in the room you upset the baby once again. Others find that it works well and after a few days to a week their baby is falling asleep with minimal crying and distress.

This is the standard method that works best for most parents, so it's the one that I cover in detail later on. Other methods are simply variations of this one – some more gentle, one more dramatic. But this is the one I strongly recommend you start off with, and then adapt depending on your baby's response.

Cry it out method

Also ominously knowns as the Extinction Method, this is the classic method that most people think of when they hear the words 'sleep training.' It may also be called 'controlled crying.' This is essentially putting your baby to bed and not returning for a long period of time, sometimes even until morning. It's hard on the baby, who may become very distressed, and it can be hard on parents too. Generally, I think it's better to accept that you are going to have a few nights of disrupted sleep attending to your baby and hopefully they will sleep better at the end of it. Most parents would find it very difficult to fall asleep to a screaming baby, anyway.

Pick up Put Down Method

This method is similar to the Fading Out method, in that you go in and out of the room for gradually lengthening periods of time. It differs, though, in that instead of reassuring your baby with words and strokes, you pick him up to soothe him, before placing him back in his cot. For some babies, this extra holding makes them feel secure and they will eventually drift off to sleep. For others, though, being picked up and put down will over time make them overstimulated and distressed, and they will fight sleep harder.

It can also depend on how you are feeling – if you find yourself getting agitated and upset by your baby's crying, he may pick up on that and become more distressed himself.

This method is, however, quite gentle, so you can start it with babies who are just a couple of months old. It may work from a very early age, and if it doesn't, you can simply try again a little later.

Camping out method

This involves being in the room, sitting on a chair, to offer reassurance, but not picking up your baby, rocking them, or feeding them. Gradually you move the chair further and further away until you are out of the room. The baby knows you are there, but gradually learns to fall asleep on her own.

This method can be used when others have failed, but can be distressing for parents if your child becomes very upset and you feel that you 'shouldn't' pick him up. However, it does mean you don't have to leave your baby alone to cry, which some parents find unbearable.

Another option here is to set up a pull out mattress next to your baby's cot, so they know you are there but can't really see you or engage with you. You can take the time to have a rest while they drift off to sleep (or bring in your smartphone, as long as your baby isn't distracted by it) and then simply tiptoe out once they are asleep. However, you may question how successful this is as your baby is still using your presence as a 'sleep aid'. It's not easy!

Sleep Training in More Detail: Here's How

I will now cover the Fade Out sleep training method, which you can adapt based on how your baby responds. This gives you a basic method to follow, but is in no way prescriptive – you'll have to adapt it to suit your temperament as well as your baby's. This is the one that trains your baby, but more gently than the traditional Cry It Out method, and seems to me the easiest on both the parents and the baby.

Here's how to do it:

1. Get your baby into his own room

If you are starting sleep training at around six months, it's fine to allow your baby to fall asleep in his own room while the training is taking place. If your baby has been in your room up until this point, leave him there, but relocate temporarily to another part of the house or apartment yourself, even on a mattress in your living room, if you have nowhere else. Once your baby is sleeping better, you can move back into your bedroom.

If your baby has been sharing a room with an older child, move the older child into your room or another room for five nights or so (let them know that it won't be forever, just until the baby is sleeping better). Once the training is over, the child can move back in with the baby – and in fact, this often works very well for young children, who like having a sibling in the same room as them.

2. Remove all sleep aids

If you want your baby to learn to sleep, you will need to remove everything that they currently use to get back to sleep. This includes pacifiers, bottles of milk, rocking and patting and breastfeeding. Babies who have learned to sleep will still wake in the night from time to time, but won't require a bottle, breastfeed, pacifier or anything else to get back to sleep. If you want a good night's sleep, all of these aids have to go, or you'll continue being woken in the night for 'room service'.

3. Plan your approach

Sleep training should ideally take place once you have worked out a plan and talked it over with your partner, so you are both on the same page. Also, if you have close neighbours, let them know what's going on so they don't assume the baby is being left to cry. Pick a time that suits you, when the baby is well and you don't have other things going on.

4. Ensure you are well and happy, too

Don't try sleep training if you are under lots of pressure at work, or don't feel happy about it for some reason. Sleep training requires calm, confident parents, so get some extra rest in preparation, and make sure you are feeling calm and positive before you start. Think Calm, Confident, Consistent and you are on your way to better nights! If you are going to be falling apart, crying and feeling guilty, it's best not to even try sleep training, as it does take determination!

The First Night

Carry out your bedtime ritual as normal around 7.30pm, ensuring your baby has been up since at least 4pm, preferably earlier.

Put her to bed without any sleep aids. She will cry, but stay out of the room for a few minutes, then go back in and provide some brief reassurance, such as a stroke of the cheek or some gentle words, then leave again.

Remember, she now needs to get herself to sleep.

Go back in to your baby as often as you need to, but gradually lengthen the intervals until she falls asleep. Be prepared for some resistance – this may take an hour, or perhaps two, and there will be a lot of crying and yelling. Remind yourself of the benefits of everyone getting more unbroken sleep at night, if you feel yourself wavering.

She will also wake up during the night, particularly if she is used to having a breastfeed, bottle or pacifier. Rather than getting up and down all night, get out of bed when she wakes again, maybe have a cup of tea or watch some TV, and wait until she goes back to sleep again.

There may be quite a lot of crying on the first night. But by the third night of sleep training there will be less, and your baby should be sleeping well within five nights, after a small amount of 'wind-down' crying at bedtime.

How to Make Sure Your Baby Sleeps Through the Night

Once you have been through sleep training with your baby, you will naturally want to make sure it continues to work. The best way to ensure your baby does a lot of sleeping and very little waking at night (allowing for the odd disruption due to sickness or a developmental leap, for example), is to stay consistent. Here are some ways to make sure your baby sleeps through the night.

Don't reintroduce sleep aids

As part of your sleep training, you removed all external sleep aids, such as pacifiers, bottles of milk, and breastfeeding. Now that you have done that, don't reintroduce the pacifier or other aids, as it will only confuse your baby and set you back.

Babies who have learned to sleep on their own, without any external help, will continue to do so, and should make it through to morning without disturbing their parents at all. This may make daytime sleeps harder for a week or so, but they will soon improve too.

Don't change their nappy during the night

Once your baby is asleep, leave them be. There is no need to change nappies during the night.

Don't panic if they vomit

Sometimes, a baby may vomit during sleep training. This is no reason to give up, as babies do vomit very easily at times. If it happens, stay calm, clean your baby without too much fuss, and continue as you started. As long as you remain calm and consistent, your baby will quickly calm down.

Why Sleep Training Fails & What to Do

Sometimes sleep training simply doesn't work. This can be due to the baby's temperament or the fact that you simply can't bear to leave your baby to cry. Here are some common reasons for failure, and what you can do about them.

- Your living arrangements aren't suitable

If you have a very small apartment and share a room with your baby, it may be difficult to leave your baby to cry. Neighbours and other people living in your house who disagree with what you're doing can also make it hard. There are no easy answers here - you may need to wait a little longer, or work on sleep training your baby a little more slowly, with less crying. Options here include rocking, patting, a dummy and breastfeeding through the night, for example.

- Your baby puts up a strong fight

Some babies will react very strongly to sleep training and giving up their sleep aids. In some cases, this may mean that it takes longer. In others, you may feel that the crying and protests aren't worth it. It may take as long as seven days to see results, but as long as you are following the guidelines I have outlined above, and your baby doesn't seem to be getting more distressed, you can continue.

It may also be that your baby isn't ready. In this case, wait until he is a little older, perhaps nine or 10 months, and then try again.

- Lack of support from those around you

Sometimes sleep training fails because one parent isn't on board with the idea, or perhaps because other people, such as well-meaning friends and family, try and tell you it's a bad idea. If you can't come to a suitable compromise, or feel yourself wavering, again, it may be better to leave it for a few months and try again later. As always, listen to your own instincts here, as they will serve you better than well-meaning outsiders who don't understand your baby or your situation as well as you do. And have a chat to your health care provider if that helps.

- Lack of planning or it's just not the right time

As you can see from reading through the programme, you need to factor in a certain amount of broken sleep and disruption when sleep training. If you try and do it at a time when you have a lot of other things happening, or you haven't factored in how much energy it will take, it may not succeed. Again (are you seeing a theme here?), let it go if it's not working or you can't handle it right now, and try again later.

Personally, I don't think it's worth doing too much sleep training before six months of age. In my experience, you will get better results if you wait until your baby is eating well during the day, and more settled generally. Before then, managing on less sleep and adapting your lifestyle accordingly is a better option.

- Lack of consistency

If you let your baby into your bed one night, then the following night refuse to pick them up, and then give up after two hours, then it's fair to say that you aren't going to successfully sleep train your baby. Remember that babies don't find it easy to understand what you are trying to do, so being consistent is essential if you want a new habit to stick. They will go along with what you want eventually, but they need to know what that is.

- You haven't got the day sleeps under control

If you don't have consistent day sleeps, you will struggle to implement any kind of routine at night. As I have stated earlier, always work on your daytime routine and your bedtime ritual before you try and tackle nights. If this is fairly consistent, sleep training should be much easier.

- Your check ups are too stimulating

When you go into to check on your baby, take care not to be too over-the-top in your attention. Remain calm and reassuring, but keep your visit as brief and simple as possible so that you don't overstimulate or further distress your baby. You want him to feel safe and reassured by your presence, but also able to put himself to sleep – a tricky balance, and one that may be easier with your second baby, if you have one.

Chapter 6 - It's Naptime!

Good day sleeps are another important need for babies through their first year. The patterns of napping will change and eventually your baby will have their own established routine. Getting this right, and prioritising naps so that they don't miss this important rest time, is key to good sleeping at night.

One question new parents often ask is if naptime can interfere with bedtime. Generally, no. While a very late nap – for example, waking up after 4pm, can lead to a later bedtime – for most babies, good naps during the day mean they aren't overtired at night and will find it easier to drift off to sleep.

If you get your baby down for his afternoon nap at time that allows for two 45-minute sleep cycles and a wake-up time of around 3pm, you should be fine for bedtime. And, of course, some lucky parents have a baby who can sleep until 5pm and still be back in bed by 7pm.

Babies change so quickly throughout their first year, and that 'good sleeper' you bring home from the hospital will soon be awake much more, and need more help to get back to sleep for daytime naps. Read on for a guide to how many naps your baby should be having throughout their first year and beyond.

Newborns (up to six weeks of age) should be having three to five naps a day, with 30 to 90 minutes awake time between each nap. There will be one nap in the morning and one or two in the afternoon, with perhaps a couple of short 'catnaps' thrown in, too.

Babies from six to 15 weeks of age should be having three to four naps a day, with one or two hours of awake time between each nap.

Babies aged four to six months need three naps a day, with lengthening awake times of 1.5 to 2.5 hours between each nap.

Babies aged six to eight months need two to three naps a day, with two to three hours of awake time between each nap.

Babies aged eight to ten months need one to two naps a day, with two to three hours between each nap. Generally, babies who wake very early (between five am and six am) will keep having two sleeps for longer. If they sleep a little later in the morning, they will transition to one sleep a day more quickly.

Babies aged 10-12 months plus need one to two naps a day, with 2.5 to 3.5 hours of awake time between each nap.

After the first birthday, your baby may continue to have two sleeps, but many will have a single, longer nap after lunch, and this can continue until they are aged three or even four. But some toddlers will drop their day sleeps quite early, which can be disappointing for parents who rely on that time to get a few things done and enjoy some peace and quiet. Read on for a few strategies to deal with babies and toddlers who refuse to nap.

Strategies for a Successful Naptime

When your baby is very small, naps will happen without you needing to do much more beyond feeding, cuddling and soothing them to sleep, perhaps in your arms or close by in bed.

You may wish to try and get them into a routine, but many parents find that their naps and awake times change so quickly that by the time they are used to one routine, their baby no longer plays along – such as when the morning nap is dropped.

Once they are around six months though, when they are settled, eating three meals and day and moving more, it can be a good idea to time daytime naps more precisely so that your baby is up and busy again well before bedtime. And, as I've mentioned earlier, sorting out your day time routine is essential for successful sleep training at night at this age.

Here are some key ways to ensure that naps are successful:

Pay attention to your baby's natural sleep cycle, and time naps accordingly.

Look for signs of tiredness – rubbing eyes, signs of unhappiness, clenched fists, avoiding eye contact – and move your baby towards their sleeping area before they get really upset, feeding first to fill them up before sleep.

Have a designated sleeping area and take them there once they are ready to nap. We have covered this already, but it should be warm but not overheated, dark, quiet and peaceful. Putting your baby to sleep in the same place for every nap may work well for babies who 'fight sleep' as it sets up strong sleep associations and signals to them that it's time for bed.

For daytime naps, a blackout blind may be helpful in encouraging your baby to drop off, and some parents swear by a strict nap schedule (for example, at 12 noon every day for exactly) to ensure that the day nap happens and bedtime isn't disrupted. As with many things, only you will be able to work out what will suit you lifestyle and your baby's temperament and sleep patterns.

Others may fall asleep in the car and readily transfer to a pram or their own bed. With my first son I used to let him fall asleep in the car, then move him gently to his pram and let him have his sleep there, so I could go to the library or a cafe and have some time to myself. This worked for me, but it won't work for all babies and toddlers, who may struggle to 'transfer' to a pram or their own bed during a nap.

Choose what works for you and your baby – the time when they are asleep is a well-deserved break for you, too, so ideally you want them to get a good, long sleep at this time so you get a break, too.

Leave them alone to fall asleep - as with sleep training at night, you sometimes need to leave your baby alone for a few minutes to actually drop off to sleep. Some babies need time to unwind and fuss a little before dropping off, so leave your baby to it and see what happens. If your baby becomes distressed, you can try picking him up, soothing etc, and then try again to put him down, drowsy and relaxed, but still awake, to see if he will fall asleep on his own.

Be consistent. Working your day around your baby's naps takes some planning, but can make life much easier. Get out and about when they are awake and happy, then be home for naptime so that they get a good long sleep and you get some time to yourself. Knowing when they need to be down for their nap so that they get a good sleep but are still up in time for their evening routine and set bedtime means that night sleeping will fall into place more easily, too.

Don't let them nap for too long, or too late. Some babies are still confused about night and day, and will sleep for too long during the day, then be alert at night. Try to limit late afternoon naps from around six months of age, getting them down for sleep earlier so you know they will have time to get through the early evening and bedtime routine without dropping off again.

While I don't believe in waking a sleeping baby (why would you?) I think it's worth timing naps so that you have some consistency when your baby will be ready for bed at night. This also ensures that your baby is getting enough sleep, which is so critical for development.

What if Your Baby Won't Nap?

Some babies and toddlers will go through tricky phases when they won't nap during the day, no matter how exhausted and grumpy they may seem. Sometimes, this can mean you need to look at bedtime and move it a little earlier or a little later and see if this helps. And some days are just more challenging than others.

If your baby hasn't had enough stimulation or exercise they may resist naptime. Here, some activity can help, such as going for a swim in a heated pool, or to a playground or playgroup. Lots of chatter, singing and engagement with them will also ready them for a good sleep. Being consistent, remaining calm and keeping an eye out for sleep cues may also help. As soon as your baby seems relaxed and drowsy, take him in to his sleeping area and see if he will drop off.

Also, some babies and toddlers will stop napping at around one year to 15 months, apart from perhaps the odd catnap. This does make the day long for parents, but if it's what your baby chooses, there's not much you can do about it. Encouraging 'quiet time' after lunch can mean you still get a break – leaving them in their room with an audio book playing, or with a few books and toys, for example. And ideally bed time will be earlier if your baby or toddler has been awake all day.

Signs that your baby or toddler is ready to drop their daytime nap are generally that the child simply refuses to sleep, even if you put him in his cot. He may play, scream or cry out. And after a week or so the parent realises the nap is not going to happen. There may be a week or two of unsettled, overtired behaviour, but eventually you and your child will both adjust to the new routine.

You may also decide to stop the daytime sleep yourself if your baby is up until 9pm at night and you are no longer getting any time to yourself in the evenings. You may choose to live with this, or you may decide to drop the daytime nap in exchange for an early bedtime – it's up to you.

If you do have a baby who doesn't sleep during the day, I recommend pursuing a sleep training programme at night. You may not be able to force your baby to sleep during the day, but that is all the more reason to assume that they can and will sleep well at night. Often, sorting out night time sleeping can help with day sleeps, too. And even if they don't, and your baby or toddler has definitely given up their day nap, or only has brief catnaps, at least everyone is getting a good sleep at night.

Remember also that so many of these problems will vanish in a few years' time and you won't even remember them. Your children will be at school, come home exhausted, and fall into bed without too much drama. So don't despair too much if you have a 'bad sleeper' – it's not your fault, and it will pass!

Chapter 7 - No Problem Too Big

In this chapter we'll cover the dreaded sleep regressions that occur as your baby moves through babyhood and toddler months. They aren't as scary as they sound, they, and will pass quickly. But until they do, there are a few things you can try that will make life easier in the meantime.

We'll also look at how to work on establishing good sleep habits when you are parenting alone. And finally, we'll cover sleep when you have twins. In both of these scenarios, parents need extra support, and there are ways of making it easier for yourself.

Understanding Sleep Regressions by Age

Sleep regression is something you will come up against a few times as your baby moves towards toddlerhood. It's totally normal, and is characterised by your baby waking up frequently when previously she had been sleeping well. Daytime naps might be difficult; you might feel like you've barely had any sleep because she was up and down all night, fretting and crying. Your baby might also seem grumpy, fretful and more clingy than usual.

Sleep regressions tend to last from about two weeks to six weeks if you're unlucky. Although sleep regression can be difficult, especially if everything has been going well up until that point, they are part of your baby's rapid development at this time, and means that they are healthy, thriving and growing as they should be.

Sleep regressions mostly occur at four, nine, 18 and 36 months of age – which are also times when your baby is changing rapidly and going through a lot of physical and cognitive development. One thing you will notice is that babies and toddlers don't change gradually – they seem the same for a while, and then all of a sudden they may be eating more, seem unsettled, or sleeping deeply, and then you'll find they have changed quite rapidly, thanks to a big growth spurt. One of the biggest transformations is around the age of three, when your toddler transforms into a very small child – and this stage is also characterised by a final sleep regression.

While not all babies and toddlers experience dramatic sleep regressions, most parents do notice a change in sleeping patterns around these ages, and it helps to be prepared for it. Read on for more information about sleep regressions by age.

The Four Month Sleep Regression

This sleep regression is when babies change from their newborn pattern of active sleep followed by deep sleep, into a new pattern of cycling through REM, light and active sleep. You may notice some unsettled behaviour and clinginess, some poor sleep at night, and also greater focus from your baby – he or she suddenly seems more alert, and more like a person. This is a lovely age and a small sleep regression won't matter so much when you noticed so much more joy and engagement from your baby!

The Nine Month Sleep Regression

The regression at nine months occurs at around the same time your baby develops "object permanence," which is the understanding that someone or something still exists even if your baby can't see them. This can also cause some separation anxiety, which is why your previously happy baby will now weep when you go to the shower, for example. Even if you have successfully sleep trained your baby at around six months, she will now wake up and realise that you're not there and start to cry, wanting you to be near her.

Let her know that you are leaving the room and will come back, rather than suddenly disappearing. This will make it easier for her and help her understand that when you go, you always come back. This may make nighttime separation anxiety less troubling, too.

Around this time babies also have a significant growth spurt as they move towards toddlerhood. They will start standing, crawling and moving around. You may notice your baby practising these skills in a half-sleep state, which obviously interferes with bedtime. Be assured, it will pass! And once they are on the move, they will sleep better at night, too.

The 18 Month Sleep Regression

This is another period of rapid change for your toddler – he or she is becoming more independent and starting to think about how he relates to others more. With a new social and emotional awareness comes increased anxiety and perhaps some disrupted sleep.

The 36 Month Sleep Regression

Much like the regression at 18 months, this period in your toddler's life is characterised by a huge leap in development and growth, both emotional and physical. Your little one may be starting pre-school, and is also likely to be talking lots, moving lots and spending time with other children more. New emotions, such as jealousy, can also take time to work through, particularly as this is often a time when a new sibling appears on the scene.

Toddlers are also learning a huge amount right now – which can make it hard for them to settle down to sleep. The world around them becomes fascinating – everything from leaves to worms to water is a source of constant information, and you'll be hearing the word 'why?'

a lot, too. Dreams and imagination are taking off, along with fears both rational and irrational.

All of these factors can increase anxiety and lead to some unsettled nights until your child settles into his new 'self.'

How to Deal With Sleep Regressions

If your baby is very young, you will need to provide extra reassurance and cuddles until the sleep regression passes. Look after your own needs, too, until your baby is more settled, and get more sleep and rest as needed, much as you did when your baby was a newborn.

If you have already sleep trained at around six months, try not to abandon everything your baby has learned. Ideally, you will provide extra care and soothing as necessary, without moving them into your bed, or giving up on letting your baby drift off to sleep alone permanently. While it may not feel like it at the time, sleep regressions do pass. Staying in the room a little longer may be all you need to do to help your baby through this stage.

If you do end up co-sleeping or cuddling your baby to sleep for a while, you may need to do some sleep training again once the regression is over – see how you go. Some tummy or head stroking, with some soothing sounds and your presence, may be all that's required, keeping to your routine of putting your baby down drowsy, but awake.

As always, keep the sleeping area dark and quiet, to give your baby the clear message that it's time to sleep. Now is a good time to demonstrate, again, that nights are a little boring, too – turn off all screens, and ensure that there's nothing too interesting happening in your house at bedtime.

Sometimes, checking in on your baby during the night and offering a stroke and a kiss may reassure them that you are there, preventing more upset later.

For sleep regressions in older babies and toddlers, also ensure that they are getting plenty of time during the day to practise new skills, such as gross motor skills. Set up an "obstacle course" in your home for them to crawl and climb over, or take them to a baby-friendly play centre and let them do some exploring. Giving them lots of opportunity to work on new skills and wear themselves out in the day time can make a big difference to your nights.

You'll also need to offer more emotional support during the day. She's feeling more adventurous and independent, but this can lead to some anxiety too. Extra attention, lots of cuddles and cosy time with books and a blanket will all make a big difference. Give her opportunities to discharge all that emotion with laughter, play and even some tears while you hold and soothe her – she'll be much happier after a good cry.

The main thing to remember is that your baby will need some extra support at this time, and the more you are able to offer, the easier and more smoothly the sleep regression will go.

If In Doubt, Seek Help

As always, if your instincts are troubling you, see your paediatrician if you feel like the sleep regression is going on for too long, or your child seems really distressed. Talking to your doctor will rule out any larger problems, and help to set your mind at ease.

Look After Yourself

If you are feeling exhausted by your child's sleep regression, be sure to cancel any unnecessary commitments and get some extra sleep yourself. As always, you need to fill your own cup up as a parent before you can take care of your child's needs properly. So eat well, have some early nights and soon it will pass.

6 Must-Know Sleep Strategies for Single Parents

If you are parenting a baby alone, first of all know that my heart goes out to you! Read on for some sleep strategies to help single parents get through those early weeks with a newborn, and through the times that follow.

Call On Help

If you can, call on family or friends to help you get through the early months with your baby. Just having someone take the baby from you for a few hours so you can get some extra sleep in the mornings will make a huge difference to your energy levels. If you can afford it, a night nurse will also be invaluable in helping you through the newborn stage. Or even someone who can come in during the day and hold the baby for a few hours, or walk it around the block, while you have a rest or just stare into space.

Gather a Support Network

If you're a single parent, you'll have times when you are managing fine, and times when you need a bit of extra help, for example when you get sick. Work on building up a reliable local support network within your community so that you can call on someone when you are having a bad week, and return the favour when they need help from you. Join online community groups, go to mother's groups, and ask your local child health centre about what kind of support is available to single parents in your area. If you have space, an au pair or student who can help out a little in exchange for accommodation is another option that may work for you.

Sleep When Your Baby Sleeps

Easier said than done, I know, particularly when you have lots of other things to do in your spare time. But worth doing for your health and your energy levels. If you don't want to sleep through every nap time, just do it when you can. Or once or twice a week, go to bed at night when your baby does, so you can catch up on sleep that way.

If you find it hard to sleep during the day, at least try and enjoy your free time when you can. Rather than doing housework, call a friend, or have a relaxing bath, or read a book with a cup of tea – whatever you need to unwind.

Consider Whether Co-sleeping Might Work For You

As we have discussed in earlier chapters, co-sleeping can often work with clingy babies who don't like to be separated from their parents. If you think this is a good idea, try setting up a cot next to your bed with an open side so your baby has a safe place to sleep, yet is still close to you. This will make nighttime feeds and wakings much easier when you don't get a respite or have someone else to share the night feeds.

Get To Know Other Single Parents

You'll soon find other people in the same position as you, who can sympathise with the challenges of lone parenting. Find groups online or in real life where you can have a laugh and talk and share tips without judgement. You're not alone – you just need to find your community! The great thing about online communities for parents is that they are global, so there's always someone to talk to, even in the middle of the night.

Be Aware of Your Mental Health

Single parenting is a tough gig at times, so it's important to be vigilant about your own health and wellbeing. Know the signs of postpartum depression, and keep in regular contact with your family doctor. Always seek help if you find yourself struggling. Keep a list of phone numbers for parenting helplines and health services close to and so you can always get support, should you need it.

Working On Your Baby's Sleep as a Single Parent

Much of what we have already covered remains the same when you are parenting alone. But here are some tips to help you with your baby's sleep that are both realistic and will make life much easier for you.

- A simple, manageable bedtime routine will help you feel in control. While this is helpful for all parents, I think it's particularly important for single parents who will find the routine stops them from being overwhelmed – and of course it's great for lone parents to get some time to themselves in the evenings, so don't feel bad about putting your baby to be early and sleep training at six months, should you need to!

- Have a sleepover with a relative or friend who can give you a break from early morning wake-ups. Ideally, it should be someone who will help out with some light housework, get up early or in the night, and provide some emotional support. One day, you will return the favour, so take all help that's offered! It's important to ask, as sometimes people don't really know what you need. And again, seek out any support services on offer within your community, too.

Two Babies, Many Solutions

If you have twins, you may be wondering if you can try sleep training at all. After all, if it's difficult to get one baby to sleep, how on earth will you manage with two? As with lone parenting, you may find that establishing and following a set routine makes it easier for you to manage this added responsibility. And again, don't be afraid to ask for help, including from local services set up to support families with twins and more. Also, take heart. While teaching two babies to sleep might seem much harder, you can and will get there. Here are some tips, often sourced from parents who have raised twins themselves.

Set the Same Bedtime for Both

What you want to do here is synchronise your babies' sleep cycles so that they are awake and asleep at around the same times. Otherwise, one or the other will always be awake, and you will soon be exhausted. Fortunately, twins are naturally in tune with one another, so here you can work with their natural inclination to be close. The principles here are much the same as sleep training single babies.

Always Settle The Calmer Baby First

You probably know this already, but if not, always work on your calmer baby first, to allow you uninterrupted time with the fussy one a little later. This will mean your calm baby gets your attention and hopefully drifts off to sleep, and therefore doesn't miss out on the attention her or she needs.

If one starts fussing, check on the quiet one first to make sure she's happy, then deal with the fussy one. This will help both babies to feel loved and happy. And don't panic if one starts screaming – often, twins aren't bothered by the other one's cry, even if they are in the same room.

Put your twins to be when they are awake, but drowsy

Here again, you can start some simple sleep training even when your twins are quite small by putting them into their safe sleeping space when they are still awake. They will hopefully drift off to sleep, leaving you with some much-needed alone time. You won't be able to rock two babies to sleep for long, so putting your babies down to sleep is going to be a decision that is made for you, to a certain degree. You can still give them cuddles while they are awake, perhaps a couple of board books and a lullaby, and soon they will learn to drift off on their own, in their own bed. Ideally your partner should be around to help with bedtimes in the early months.

Try Swaddling Your Babies

Swaddling can work well for all babies, but is particularly helpful when it works for twins (I say when, because not all babies like being swaddled.) It makes babies feel safe, 'held,' and ready for sleep, and they are after all used to being very tightly packed into a small space! You will need to stop at around two months of age, but at this point you can swap to zip-up baby sleeping bags for the same sleep association and secure feeling.

Keep Nights Boring and Quiet

As with all babies, you want to discourage them from seeing night as anything other than a time to sleep. During the day, cuddle and talk to them as much as you like. But keep night-time interactions, light, cuddles and chatter to a minimum, so they are clear on the fact that nights are not play time. This is important with all babies, but particularly important with twins, when you have two babies to settle, not just one. Twins may also like a cuddly toy or some comfort object to hold onto at night from around one year of age.

Black-out blinds, lullaby CDs and white noise machines are another thing that may twin parents find very handy when getting two babies to sleep. Draw on everything you can find, and you'll find it much easier!

Accept That Your Twins May Have Different Sleep Needs

If you find that your twins sleep differently, which is common, you may need to treat them differently. Some parents put their twins in separate rooms, as one is a better sleeper than the other. As with all aspects of parenting, as long is it's safe, it's up to you. One waking up is always better than two waking up, so whatever works!

You may need to separate them into separate rooms to sleep train at around six months, and then put them back in the same room once you've managed this and they are sleeping well again. Or you might get them to sleep each night in separate rooms and then move them into one room later on in the night – up to you. The sooner you get them sleeping in a way that will work for you all long term, the better for your family as a whole. As always, go easy on yourself and ask for help when you need it.

With daytime naps, it may be that you need to soothe one to sleep first, and then the other, so one wakes around around 20 minutes earlier than the second. This is part of life with twin babies – to some extent you need to be flexible and let go of expectations. You just need to do everything one baby at a time and be patient. It will get easier!

Set Up A Sleep Schedule

More so than with one baby, with twins it's absolutely critical that parents are getting enough sleep. It shouldn't be one person getting up to do all the night wakings, it should be both. Setting up a timetable or schedule will help to ensure that no one becomes too sleep deprived. Obviously you'll need to take into account the needs of your own family, and work commitments.

Call in Help

If you can afford it, get some help, particularly in the early days. A night nurse, a cleaner, even someone to cook a few healthy meals – whatever it takes to get you through. A live-in au pair is another option that can work well.

Online parenting forums specifically for twins are another invaluable source of tips and support, as are multiple birth associations, so get on board with all of these as soon as you know you are expecting twins.

Streamline Everything

Have as much done in advance as you can – for example, bottles sterilised, nappies stocked up, sleeping bags laid out before you bring each baby out of the bath at night. Meal plan, have a weekly online shop, get regular help… whatever it takes to simplify your life! And be sure to schedule in some time for yourself, too – when you are parenting twins, this isn't a luxury, it's essential.

Chapter 8 - Completing Your No-Cry Toolkit

In our final chapter, we'll look at some common problems that come up with babies, and how you can work through them. These include how to soothe a crying baby – giving you lots of hints and strategies. We'll also look at colic – what it is, what helps, and how you can help your baby work through it. And finally, we'll look at how you can help your baby sleep better when he or she is not feeling well.

How to Soothe a Crying Baby

Learning to soothe a crying baby is something you learn on the job, and when you have a baby who cries a lot, it can be very tough on a new parent. You may wonder what's wrong with your baby, or that you are going to lose control and harm your baby or that you aren't connecting with your baby. I remember fearing, as a very new mother, that my baby was scared of me and that was why he was crying! It can feel like a rejection, but it really isn't. It's simply your baby getting used to being in the world. Once you establish some basic feeding and sleeping routines, and your baby is a little bigger, it will all get much easier.

In the meantime, learning a few techniques to soothe a crying baby will help you get through the bad days. Firstly, let's look at why babies cry so much, as this knowledge can help parents feel better able to manage it and not feel overwhelmed.

So why do babies cry so much?

All babies cry. But in truth, no one can say for sure exactly why babies. It may be to do with hunger, or bellyaches, or overtiredness. They can't talk, so they can't tell us exactly what the problem is, unfortunately. Crying is their way of gaining our attention and focus, which they need to survive when they are so small and helpless. But over time, you will learn to recognise some of your baby's unique crying patterns and what they mean – and then you will be able to meet their needs so the crying soon stops.

And in fact, it's important to remember that a healthy baby should and will cry regularly. If your baby never cries, you should seek advice from your family doctor.

Some common reasons for crying include:
- Tiredness and overstimulation; need for sleep
- Needing a new diaper
- Feeling hungry
- Colic, reflux or food intolerances
- Pain or sickness
- Gas
- Fear or a sudden loud noise may lead to crying
- No apparent reason

As a parent, it can be hard to deal with a crying baby for hours on end, particularly when you are tired and emotional yourself. But a certain amount of crying is completely normal for all babies, and some cry a lot more than others.

What you need to bear in mind, too, is that excessive crying can be very hard on you as a parent, especially if you are someone who tends to be quite hard on yourself. You may feel that you 'should' be able to deal with your baby and you are doing something wrong if you can't stop him crying. But in fact, by simply being there, holding your baby and letting him know you are there, you are doing everything right. The early days and weeks where there may be a lot of crying will soon pass and in the meantime, you just need to go easy on yourself and get as much rest as you can. Unexplained crying builds from birth, tends to peak at about six weeks of age, and tapers off by three months. Mark your calendar and look forward to that magic date when the crying stops – it will come.

Having said that, if your baby seems like they are in pain, or you sense that something is wrong, always seek medical help. Trust your instincts.

Baby Crying Patterns by Age

Birth to three weeks: At this age, many babies sleep a lot and cry for only short periods of time, usually due to hunger or tiredness.

Three weeks to 12 weeks: At this point, babies tend to cry more and sleep less. There may be some periods of crying due to hunger or overtiredness, which are easily solved with sleep, a feed or some gentle soothing. And there may be some periods of unexplained crying where nothing seems to help. For some babies, there is a lot of crying, for no apparent reason, that goes on for a few months, often until three or six months of age. This occurs with around 20 per cent of babies, unfortunately. By six months, most babies are much happier and more settled in the world.

Often the diagnosis is 'colic', which is a kind of catch-all term for the unsettled crying and apparent stomach pain that many babies seem to show when they crying a lot, writhe and howl after feeding. Often, there may be more crying in the evening, that can go on for a couple of hours before sleep descends. And sometimes there may be a bad day when it feels like your baby does nothing but cry.

Here are some effective remedies for colic that you may find useful. There are no proven treatments for colic, because the causes can be so hard to pinpoint in individual babies, mostly because they are so young and change so quickly. But you can try and lesson their discomfort and distress so that the episode passes more quickly, and in trying different things you may be able to pinpoint what is causing them it to some extent.

5 Effective Remedies for Colic

Lay your baby on his tummy

You can do this across your lap, on the floor on a rug, or more upright along your chest. You can also gently rub his back, which might help with any digestive discomfort. Tummy time will also help to strengthen neck and shoulder muscles, but you should only do this when your baby is awake and you are there to keep an eye on him or he

Work on good sleep

Of course I would say this! But it's true – sorting out good sleep is the key to sorting out a lot of your baby's unsettled behaviour. And very small babies have an added difficulty in that they find it hard to 'hold still' enough to go to sleep, often jerking themselves awake as they drop off. Swaddling, rocking and even "wearing" your baby in a sling are all ways to hold them still enough to soothe their distress and let them fall asleep. Another trick is to walk the floor with your baby – wrap them up or put them in a sling, and the pace up and down until they drop off. If you know they are well fed and there aren't any underlying health issues, it's fine to wear headphones may block out the crying until they fall asleep.

Another problem is of course that babies can only stay away for a short period of time before they get grumpy and restless, and they then need to calm down enough to fall asleep – but are crying too much to manage this! This is something that they will learn to do over time, and meanwhile they need your patience and support.

Introduce a pacifier

You may find that your baby is much happier and able to calm themselves down with a pacifier. Yes, you will need to get rid of it at some point, but many parents find it gives them some much needed relief from crying.

Give a warm bath before bed

A long, warm bath will often calm a crying baby – the water, the sounds and the soothing hands holding them will all help to settle colic and fretful behaviour. A massage in dark, warm room with a scented oil, some cuddling, and gentle white noise may also help to soothe a colicky baby.

Gentle handling

When your baby is very unhappy and colicky, be sure to handle them with firm, steady movements, without any jerking or hard back-patting. Sharp movements will alarm your baby and cause more screaming and upset. Another reason small babies become upset is if they are handed between lots of different people. Sometimes, if your baby becomes overstimulated retreating to a dark, quiet room can help. What they need more than anything is a calm, safe environment with you. They have just arrived in the world, after all, and it can be frightening.

Oddly enough, some parents report that holding their baby a lot during the day gives rise to easier evenings. Babies love being held, rocked, and close to you, so if you leave them in their pram all day they may "hand you a bill" later and demand a few hours of your undivided attention in the evening. If you find you have a very clingy, colicky baby, a sling can help you get a few things done without having to put your baby down.

An important point: This need for attention never really goes away – your children will always want your attention, and pre-empting this need with lots of loving attention will prevent them trying to gain it with acting out, or giving up and "looking for love in all the wrong places" later on.

Manage your own wellbeing with a colicky baby

When it comes to colicky babies, it's also helpful to manage this phase (which won't last long, but may feel like it's going to last for ever) by taking good care of yourself. Ask for support and help from those you trust, who won't make comments about your howling baby, and take any food, babysitting offers or help with cleaning that comes your way.

- Do you have someone who can come over and just hold the baby for a while so you can have a shower and some time to yourself?

- Can you get a cleaner or some other help with housework so you don't have to live in a mess, which can be very stressful?

- Can you put in some headphones and let the baby cry for a while in his bed while you take a bit of time out? A healthy baby can be left to cry for short periods of time quite safely, and may even drop off to sleep if left alone.

- Look after yourself. A crying baby can be exhausting, so as always, prioritise your own wellbeing and you will feel better able to cope with your baby. Eat well, get enough rest, and avoid alcohol and smoking and you will feel better able to cope with this stage in your life.

Is it a medical problem?

No one really knows. Some babies may suffer from reflux or other stomach upsets or be particularly sensitive to a particular formula milk, or something their mother has eaten if they are breastfed. Some mothers may try eliminating certain foods, such as chillies, spicy food, coffee, garlic or dairy – there's no harm in trying and seeing what happens.

Helping a Sick Baby Get Restful Sleep

Another aspect of living with a baby that you will have to get used to is occasional sickness, at least until their immune system has built up a little. The first year of daycare can also be rough, as your baby will bring home lots of bugs and germs he hasn't been exposed to before. Lack of hygiene and a tendency to explore and put fingers in mouths also leads to lots of not-so-lovely germs being shared around. You might noticed earaches (lots of screaming and head-banging), colds, blocked noses, feverishness and upset stomachs.

Of course, most serious illnesses can be prevented by immunisation, but colds and sniffles will still appear, and can also lead to some broken nights, sadly. Often, a sick baby will be in pain and will find it impossible to sleep. Yet sleep is exactly what they need to fight off illness and recover. What you need to do is decrease their discomfort to the point that they can sleep soundly without aches and pains keeping them (and you) up.

Here are some ways you can help your baby or toddler get a good night's sleep when they are ill:

- Use a humidifier. This will ease breathing difficulties and reduce the chance of your baby waking up due to congestion.
- Use an over-the-counter painkiller for children. Talk to your pharmacist about the best one to use and follow the instructions for correct dosages very carefully. Some babies and toddlers will happily swallow a liquid treatment, others may need a suppository. Never give more than the recommended dose – keep note of how much you have given and when.
- Allow for extra naps in the daytime to make up for broken sleep at night. Extra rocking, cuddling and attention is also going to help your baby feel better, as sickness can make them miserable and clingy. On the same note, start the bedtime routine a little earlier and make sure your baby doesn't get cold when you bathe him or her – keep a towel in the bathroom and dress him there straight away to prevent chills, and make the water nice and steamy to help clear his nose. Sometimes, sitting in a steamy bathroom can help, too.
- A vapor rub on his chest can ease breathing and feels nice, too. You can make your own by mixing up four teaspoons of grated beeswax with three tablespoons of cocoa or shea butter, seven tablespoons of coconut oil and 30 drops off essential oil – ten drops eucalyptus oil, ten drops tea tree oil, five drops lavender oil and five drops chamomile oil is a lovely blend that will clear a blocked nose and promote sleep.
- Saline nose drops, available from the pharmacist, can help to clear a blocked nose, though your baby may protest loudly.
- Propping up your baby's mattress slightly, by putting a pillow under the mattress, will also help to ease a blocked nose and the pain of an ear infection. Only do this with babies that are six months old and upwards.

- Keep your baby hydrated, either with extra breastfeeds or bottles, as needed. Older babies might prefer watered-down juice or milk – whatever keeps them drinking fluid.
- If your baby vomits in bed, clean her up as quickly and calmly as you can, keeping lights low if possible. You may also like to clean out her mouth a little to get rid of the bad taste.
- Extra skin-to-skin contact is very good for sick babies, and is proven to speed up recovery. Hold your baby against your skin and remember that she will soon feel better.

Once the sickness passed

You may need to work a little to get back into your old sleep routine, but don't let all your progress be undone by a single bout of illness. Once your baby is feeling better, go back to leaving him to fall asleep in his cot, even if you've been rocking him to sleep during his illness. Babies are fast learners and you should be able to get back on track quickly as long as you remain calm and consistent.

Preventing another illness

While illness is simply part of childhood, and something you have to accept to some degree, you also want to prevent your child catching a serious illness that will affect his development. Here are some tips to prevent illness from rearing its head too often:

- First and most importantly, immunise your child according to his schedule. This is the best, and sometimes the only way to prevent serious childhood illnesses such as measles, mumps and rubella.
- Be sure to live in a smoke-free home and avoid smoke-filled areas to keep your children's lungs clear.

- Always wash your hands when you get home from anywhere. Over time, your child will watch you and will become a good hand washer on their own. Provide a stool in the bathroom so your child can access water and soap easily.
- Wash towels, sheets and all bedding frequently.
- Avoid sharing cups, cutlery and so on.
- Breastfeeding for the first 12 months is a great way to pass on your own immunity to germs that you encounter.
- Eat lots of fresh fruit and vegetables to boost immunity. Once your baby is moving onto solids, ensure their diet is full of vitamins, too.
- If your child is sick, don't go to playdates, playgrounds or public places such as libraries. Stay at home until it passes and don't spread the germs.
- Remember that childhood illness is normal and part of your baby building up his immune system – it will pass.

A final point: Sometimes, sleep problems can feel insurmountable. Let's say you've read this entire book, tried everything I have recommended, and your baby is still not sleeping well. As I have said throughout, this will change with time. But if you find you are feeling continually worried and stressed about your baby's lack of sleep, and the impact it is having on your, don't be afraid to seek help from a child health expert, such as your family doctor.

Occasionally, sleep problems can point to wider problems within the family, or even post-natal depression, and you will need to deal with these issues before you tackle sleep. If this rings true for you, and you've found it impossible to put into place a sleep training method, then perhaps you need to seek further help. It is there if you need it.

But generally, like everything to do with babies and toddlers, as long as the basics are there – lots of love, patience, support for parents and an understanding of baby and toddler behaviour – sleep should fall into place, if not straight away, then eventually. In the meantime, look after yourself at all times, because as a parent, your little one depends on your completely, and your health and wellbeing is the foundation of stable, thriving family life.

Conclusion

I hope this book has given you a lot to work with, and you now feel ready to handle your baby's sleep problems and to attempt sleep training if you feel it's the best option for your family. As you can see, there are no perfect solutions when it comes to baby and toddler sleep, and I have tried at all times to emphasise that this is a stage that will pass, and as a parent you are well-equipped to find your own ways to manage. Some toddlers and babies are just better sleepers than others – it's often a matter of luck, but you can improve things with some work and planning.

We looked first as sleep patterns by age, and what is normal for each stage. This is great for helping you see that what may feel like problems are actually totally normal and will pass with time. We also looked at how to set up a safe sleeping space for your baby, which is more important than anything else. Here we also covered sleep aids, such as monitors, night lights, blackout blinds and white noise machines, and when these might be a good idea.

Next we covered sleep associations – what they are and how to create them. And we looked at a basic routine that you can put in place to help with good sleeping, both during the day and at night. As always, a busy day and a structured, loving and fun routine is ideal for creating the right conditions for peaceful night sleeping.

In chapter three, we looked at sleep problems by age, both common and less common, and then we moved onto sleep training in chapter four, and how to choose the right method for your baby. We also covered tips for success, and how you might decide that the time is right for sleep training, such as if you are returning to work or you are simply feeling exhausted and want to tackle sleep problems a little.

We also looked at why six months is the perfect time to first try sleep training. You now know that the longer a baby or toddler is used to behaving in a certain way, such as being rocked to sleep, the more they will struggle to give it up. By the time a toddler is two, getting him to stop falling asleep in your bed, or on the couch, is going to be a lot harder. Changing the routine later on is going to involve a lot more resistance, and a lot more pain. Having said that, if you remain calm and consistent, sleep training will usually succeed at any age. It's just that six months is the first and often the best time to try it. After that, as your baby turns into a toddler, it may not be quite so easy, and your child will also be able to climb out of their cot and use their words to make you feel like a terrible parent, so it may be better to start sooner!

Next, we dived into the main techniques for sleep training – Fading Out, Crying it Out, Pick Up Put Down and Camping Out. We looked at which babies (and parents) are best suited to each method, and why Fading Out is the one that is most likely to succeed for many families. We then looked at why, unfortunately, sleep training might fail, and what to do if that happens. Often, it's simply a case of trying again later. And, remember, as always, that if it doesn't work, or you find it too hard, then you may go back to whatever you've been doing and forget about it entirely, knowing that you tried. As the parent, it's your call.

In Chapter Six we covered nap times for different ages, and why good daytime naps are key to sound sleeping at night. We also looked at what to do if your baby won't nap. Next we moved on to sleep regression, and how to handle them at each stage, and importantly, why they happen. As with so much of parenting, knowing what is developmentally normal can make it a lot easier to deal with. Here, we also looked at how single parents, and those look after twins, can manage sleep, naps and parenting in general – the two key tips here, and for all parents, are to look after yourself and seek help if you need to.

Lastly, we looked at crying babies – what crying means, how to soothe it, how to deal with colic in the early weeks. We then covered how to manage sickness and sleep, and how to prevent childhood illness as much as possible.

I hope that you now have a lot of information and confidence to deal with your baby's sleep. While there is no magic secret to great sleep in the early months, there is a lot you can do to move things in the right direction. Try not to beat yourself up, though, if you find it difficult coping on broken sleep while also trying to get on with other elements of your life, such as work and other relationships. It's normal, in the early years, to be functioning on very little sleep and not feeling full of energy, and many other parents are in the same boat. If anything, these years will teach you to be a little bit more understanding of those around you who seem tired and out of sorts – they may well have a very small baby at home, keeping them up at night.

Good luck, and enjoy the journey!